Blockchain Bedtime Stories

Book 1

Randall Campbell

Randall Campbell

© 2024 Blckswmngbrd llc. All rights reserved.

No part of this publication may be reproduced, distributed, or transmitted in any form or by any means, including photocopying, recording, or other electronic or mechanical methods, without the prior written permission of the publisher, except in the case of brief quotations embodied in critical reviews and certain other noncommercial uses permitted by copyright law. For permission requests, write to the publisher at the address below.

contact@blckswmngbrd.com

Blockchain Bedtime Stories

"By convention, the first transaction in a block is a special transaction that starts a new coin owned by the creator of the block."

Satoshi Nakamoto

Table of Contents

Proof of Work Quest...13
    Explanation of Concepts 17
    Questions 19
    Answers 20

Trusted Hands Rise 21
    Explanation of Concepts 25
    Questions 27
    Answers 28

Byzantine Puzzle..29
    Explanation of Concepts 33
    Questions 35
    Answers 36

Rules Written Openly...37
    Explanation of Concepts 41
    Questions 43
    Answers 44

Off-Chain Council 45
Explanation of Concepts 49
Questions 51
Answers 52
Cross-Chain Conundrum 53
Explanation of Concepts 57
Questions 59
Answers 60
Protocols of Connectivity 61
Explanation of Concepts 65
Questions 67
Answers 68
Three Tokens of Power 69
Explanation of Concepts 73
Questions 75
Answers 76
Supply Side Tales 77
Explanation of Concepts 81
Questions 83
Answers 84
Scarcity Sparks Value 85
Explanation of Concepts 89
Questions 91

Answers 92
Unveiling the Network's Hidden Dangers 93
    Explanation of Concepts 97
    Questions 99
    Answers 100
Forging the Network's Shield 102
    Explanation of Concepts 107
    Questions 109
    Answers 110
Cloaked in Coins 111
    Explanation of Concepts 115
    Questions 117
    Answers 118
Hushed Transactions 119
    Explanation of Concepts 123
    Questions 125
    Answers 126
Stable Shifts Ahead 127
    Explanation of Concepts 131
    Questions 133
    Answers 134
Taming the Tokens 135
    Explanation of Concepts 139

  Questions 141

  Answers 142

Hat Tricks & Tokens **143**

  Explanation of Concepts 147

  Questions 149

  Answers 150

Magic in the Digital Gallery **151**

  Explanation of Concepts 155

  Questions 156

  Answers 158

Tokens of Change **159**

  Explanation of Concepts 163

  Questions 165

  Answers 166

Autonomy Unfurled **168**

  Explanation of Concepts 172

  Questions 174

  Answers 175

Bearly Decentralized **177**

  Explanation of Concepts 182

  Questions 184

  Answers 185

Hashing Insights **187**

>   Explanation of Concepts 191
>
>   Questions 193
>
>   Answers 194
>
> **Chains of Trust** **196**
>
>   Explanation of Concepts 200
>
>   Questions 202
>
>   Answers 203
>
> **Squirrels Solve Puzzles** **205**
>
>   Explanation of Concepts 209
>
>   Questions 211
>
>   Answers 212
>
> **Blocks of Wisdom** **214**
>
>   Explanation of Concepts 218
>
>   Questions 220
>
>   Answers 221
>
> **Self-Executing Scrolls** **223**
>
>   Explanation of Concepts 227
>
>   Questions 229
>
>   Answers 230
>
> **Forked Paths Ahead** **231**
>
>   Explanation of Concepts 235
>
>   Questions 237
>
>   Answers 238

Mining for Knowledge 239
    Explanation of Concepts 243
    Questions 245
    Answers 246

Enlightened by Ethereum 247
    Explanation of Concepts 251
    Questions 253
    Answers 255

Alternatives and Variety 256
    Explanation of Concepts 260
    Questions 262
    Answers 263

Tokens Transform Friends 265
    Explanation of Concepts 269
    Questions 271
    Answers 272

Purses, Keys, and Wallets 274
    Explanation of Concepts 278
    Questions 280
    Answers 282

Keys Open Doors 283
    Explanation of Concepts 287
    Questions 289

Answers 290

Public Service Addresses 291

Explanation of Concepts 295

Questions 297

Answers 298

Enchanted Address Quest 299

Explanation of Concepts 303

Questions 305

Answers 307

An Equivalent Exchange 308

Explanation of Concepts 312

Questions 314

Answers 315

Unforgiving Marketplaces 317

Explanation of Concepts 321

Questions 323

Answers 324

Liquid Pool of Treasures 325

Explanation of Concepts 329

Questions 331

Answers 332

Case of the Magical Harvest 333

Explanation of Concepts 337

Questions 339
Answers 340

Stakes in the Evergreen Forest 341
Explanation of Concepts 345
Questions 347
Answers 348

Lending Library of Evergreen Forest 349
Explanation of Concepts 353
Questions 355
Answers 356

Leaf it to Us 357
Explanation of Concepts 361
Questions 363
Answers 364

Fuel for Thought 365
Explanation of Concepts 369
Questions 371
Answers 372

Quest for Satoshi's Treasure 373
Explanation of Concepts 378
Questions 380
Answers 381

Bear with Blockchains 382

Explanation of Concepts 386
Questions 388
Answers 390

Proof of Work Quest

A cluster of berries tumbled down a hill, scattering in all directions. Robbie Rabbit darted after them, scooping up the juicy treats with glee.

"Forget the berries, Barry! We've got a new quest from the Wise Old Wizard!" Robbie exclaimed, waving a scroll enthusiastically.

Barry Bear, who had just finished organizing his honey jars, looked up. "What now, Robbie?"

"It's called Proof of Work! The Wizard wants us to understand how it works and its importance!" Robbie said, hopping excitedly.

"Proof of Work? Sounds interesting," Barry replied, already curious.

They made their way to the Wise Old Wizard's tower, where the Wizard greeted them warmly, his eyes twinkling with knowledge.

"Ah, Barry and Robbie, welcome," the Wizard began. "Today, we will explore the world of Proof of Work, or PoW, a system that ensures security and integrity in our enchanted network."

Barry tilted his head. "How does PoW work?"

The Wizard nodded. "Proof of Work is a consensus mechanism where participants solve complex puzzles to validate transactions and secure the network (puzzle-solving). It's like a grand competition where the first to solve the puzzle gets to add the next block to the chain."

Robbie's ears perked up. "So, it's a bit like a race?"

"Exactly, Robbie," the Wizard replied. "The process of solving these puzzles is known as mining, and it requires significant computational power and energy (mining)."

With a wave of the Wizard's staff, a shimmering portal opened, leading them into a vibrant mine bustling with activity.

"First, let's explore how mining works," the Wizard said, leading them to a large cavern filled with creatures working on intricate puzzles. "Miners compete to solve cryptographic puzzles. The first to solve it gets to add a new block of transactions to the ledger and is rewarded for their effort (block reward)."

Barry watched as a fox solved a puzzle and received a gleaming reward. "So, they get paid for their work?"

"Precisely, Barry," the Wizard replied. "This incentivizes miners to continue securing the network and processing transactions."

Robbie hopped around the cavern. "What happens if someone tries to cheat?"

The Wizard smiled. "If a miner attempts to cheat, their puzzle solution will be invalid, and they won't be able to add the block. This system of validation ensures that only legitimate transactions are recorded (validation)."

They moved on to a bustling marketplace where creatures traded various goods. "Now, let's explore some use cases and projects using PoW," the Wizard announced.

Barry saw a group of pixies managing a bustling trading platform. "What's this?"

"That's Bitcoin," the Wizard explained. "Bitcoin uses PoW to secure its network and ensure that all transactions are legitimate. Miners validate transactions by solving puzzles, which keeps the network running smoothly (Bitcoin)."

Robbie sniffed the air. "Smells like opportunity!"

The Wizard chuckled. "Indeed, Robbie. Another example is Ethereum, which initially used PoW to manage and secure its smart contracts and decentralized applications. Miners played a crucial role in maintaining the network's integrity (Ethereum)."

Next, they arrived at a serene lake where creatures mined precious stones. "This is Litecoin," the Wizard said. "Litecoin uses PoW for faster transaction times and lower fees. It's similar to Bitcoin but optimized for everyday transactions (Litecoin)."

Barry's eyes widened. "That's incredible! What else?"

The Wizard led them to a bustling workshop where creatures crafted unique items. "This is Monero," the

Wizard explained. "Monero uses PoW to ensure privacy and security for its users. It's designed to keep transactions confidential and untraceable (Monero)."

Robbie clapped his paws. "This place is amazing! Anything else?"

The Wizard nodded. "There's also Dogecoin, which started as a joke but gained popularity for its friendly community and efficient transactions. It uses PoW to maintain security and encourage participation (Dogecoin)."

Barry and Robbie spent the rest of the day exploring the world of PoW, amazed by its efficiency and the innovative projects built within it. By the time the sun began to set, they felt enlightened and excited about the endless possibilities.

As they made their way back through the portal, Robbie couldn't help but make Barry laugh with his impressions of the Wise Old Wizard explaining PoW's wonders.

Barry, feeling wiser and more connected, knew that with the power of PoW, they could explore and innovate in ways they had never imagined.

Explanation of Concepts

1. **Puzzle-Solving**: Proof of Work (PoW) is a consensus mechanism where participants solve complex puzzles to validate transactions and secure the network. It's a competitive process where the first to solve the puzzle gets to add the next block to the chain.
2. **Mining**: The process of solving these puzzles in PoW is known as mining. It requires significant computational power and energy. Miners compete to solve cryptographic puzzles, and the first to solve it gets to add a new block of transactions to the ledger and is rewarded for their effort.
3. **Block Reward**: Miners are rewarded for their efforts with new tokens or coins. This incentivizes them to continue securing the network and processing transactions. The reward system ensures that miners are compensated for their work in maintaining the network.
4. **Validation**: In PoW, if a miner attempts to cheat, their puzzle solution will be invalid, and they won't be able to add the block. This system of validation ensures that only legitimate transactions are recorded, maintaining the integrity of the network.
5. **Bitcoin**: Bitcoin uses PoW to secure its network and ensure that all transactions are legitimate. Miners validate transactions by solving puzzles, which keeps the network running smoothly and securely.

6. **Ethereum**: Initially used PoW to manage and secure its smart contracts and decentralized applications. Miners played a crucial role in maintaining the network's integrity by validating transactions and securing the blockchain.
7. **Litecoin**: Uses PoW for faster transaction times and lower fees compared to Bitcoin. It's designed for everyday transactions, offering a more efficient and accessible network for users.
8. **Monero**: Uses PoW to ensure privacy and security for its users. It's designed to keep transactions confidential and untraceable, offering a high level of privacy for all network participants.
9. **Dogecoin**: Started as a joke but gained popularity for its friendly community and efficient transactions. It uses PoW to maintain security and encourage participation, making it a fun and accessible cryptocurrency.

Questions

1. What is Proof of Work (PoW) primarily used for?

    A. Making coins

    B. Solving puzzles to validate transactions and secure the network

    C. Building houses

    D. Growing crops

2. What do miners receive as a reward for solving puzzles in a Proof of Work system?

    A. A special key

    B. New tokens or coins (Block Reward)

    C. Magic powers

    D. Access to hidden treasure

3. Which cryptocurrency originally used Proof of Work to secure smart contracts and decentralized applications?

    A. Bitcoin

    B. Monero

    C. Ethereum

    D. Dogecoin

4. What is a key feature of Monero that distinguishes it from other cryptocurrencies using PoW?

A. Faster transaction times

B. Focus on privacy and untraceable transactions

C. It started as a joke

D. It uses no energy

5. If a miner attempts to cheat by providing an invalid puzzle solution in PoW, what happens?

A. Their puzzle solution is accepted

B. They receive extra rewards

C. Their solution is invalid, and they cannot add the block

D. They automatically win the game

Answers

1. **B** - Solving puzzles to validate transactions and secure the network
2. **B** - New tokens or coins (Block Reward)
3. **C** - Ethereum
4. **B** - Focus on privacy and untraceable transactions
5. **C** - Their solution is invalid, and they cannot add the block

Trusted Hands Rise

A flash of sunlight caught on a shiny pebble, casting a dazzling array of colors across the forest clearing. Robbie Rabbit, ever curious, pounced on it with great excitement.

"Barry! You won't believe what I've found!" Robbie exclaimed, waving a scroll triumphantly.

Barry Bear, organizing his honey jars, glanced up. "What is it this time, Robbie?"

"It's a message from the Wise Old Wizard! He wants us to learn about Proof of Authority!" Robbie's enthusiasm was infectious.

"Proof of Authority? That sounds intriguing," Barry replied, already interested.

They made their way to the Wise Old Wizard's tower, where the Wizard greeted them warmly, his eyes twinkling with knowledge.

"Ah, Barry and Robbie, welcome," the Wizard began. "Today, we will explore the concept of Proof of Authority, or PoA, a system that ensures trust and efficiency in our enchanted network."

Barry tilted his head. "How does PoA work?"

The Wizard nodded. "Proof of Authority is a consensus mechanism where a limited number of approved participants, called validators, are responsible for verifying transactions and maintaining the network (validators). It's like having a council of trusted elders who oversee the community."

Robbie's ears perked up. "So, it's like having guardians?"

"Exactly, Robbie," the Wizard replied. "These validators are chosen based on their identity and reputation, ensuring that they have a vested interest in acting honestly and efficiently (identity-based selection)."

With a wave of the Wizard's staff, a shimmering portal opened, leading them into a vibrant town hall bustling with activity.

"First, let's explore how validators work in PoA," the Wizard said, leading them to a grand council chamber. "Here, validators are pre-approved and trusted by the community to validate transactions. This makes the system efficient and fast, as there is no need for complex calculations to validate blocks (efficiency)."

Barry watched as a wise owl validated a transaction with a simple gesture. "So, it's quicker than other systems?"

"Precisely, Barry," the Wizard replied. "Because the validators are known and trusted, the process is streamlined, making transactions faster and more efficient."

Robbie hopped around the chamber. "What if a validator tries to cheat?"

The Wizard smiled. "If a validator acts dishonestly, their reputation and authority are at risk. The community can replace them with someone more trustworthy, ensuring accountability (accountability)."

They moved on to a bustling marketplace where creatures traded various goods. "Now, let's explore some use cases and projects using PoA," the Wizard announced.

Barry saw a group of pixies managing a bustling trading platform. "What's this?"

"That's VeChain," the Wizard explained. "VeChain uses PoA to manage and track supply chains efficiently. Validators ensure that all transactions are accurate and trustworthy, which is crucial for maintaining the integrity of supply chains (VeChain)."

Robbie sniffed the air. "Smells like opportunity!"

The Wizard chuckled. "Indeed, Robbie. Another example is xDai, a stablecoin platform that uses PoA to provide fast and low-cost transactions. Validators ensure that payments are processed quickly and reliably, making it ideal for everyday transactions (xDai)."

Next, they arrived at a serene garden where creatures collaborated on projects. "This is POA Network," the Wizard said. "It's a platform that uses PoA to offer scalability and interoperability for decentralized applications. Validators help ensure the network runs smoothly and securely (POA Network)."

Barry's eyes widened. "That's incredible! What else?"

The Wizard led them to a bustling port where creatures exchanged various assets. "This is Kovan," the Wizard explained. "Kovan is a test network for Ethereum that uses PoA. It allows developers to test their applications in a controlled environment before deploying them on the main network (Kovan)."

Robbie clapped his paws. "This place is amazing! Anything else?"

The Wizard nodded. "There's also Azure Blockchain, a platform by Microsoft that uses PoA to offer enterprise solutions. Validators ensure that the network is secure and efficient, making it suitable for business applications (Azure Blockchain)."

Barry and Robbie spent the rest of the day exploring the world of PoA, amazed by its efficiency and the innovative projects built within it. By the time the sun began to set, they felt enlightened and excited about the endless possibilities.

As they made their way back through the portal, Robbie couldn't help but make Barry laugh with his impressions of the Wise Old Wizard explaining PoA's wonders.

Barry, feeling wiser and more connected, knew that with the power of PoA, they could explore and innovate in ways they had never imagined.

Explanation of Concepts

1. **Validators**: In Proof of Authority (PoA), validators are a limited number of approved participants responsible for verifying transactions and maintaining the network. They are chosen based on their identity and reputation, ensuring they act honestly and efficiently.
2. **Identity-Based Selection**: Validators in PoA are selected based on their known identity and reputation. This ensures that those chosen have a vested interest in maintaining the integrity and efficiency of the network, as their reputation is at stake.
3. **Efficiency**: PoA is an efficient system because the validators are known and trusted, eliminating the need for complex calculations to validate transactions. This streamlines the process, making it faster and more cost-effective than other consensus mechanisms.
4. **Accountability**: If a validator in a PoA system acts dishonestly, their reputation and authority are at risk. The community can replace them with someone more trustworthy, ensuring that validators remain accountable and the network remains secure.
5. **VeChain**: VeChain uses PoA to manage and track supply chains efficiently. Validators ensure that all transactions are accurate and trustworthy, maintaining the integrity of the supply chain data.
6. **xDai**: xDai is a stablecoin platform that uses PoA to provide fast and low-cost transactions. Validators

ensure that payments are processed quickly and reliably, making it ideal for everyday transactions and microtransactions.
7. **POA Network**: A platform that uses PoA to offer scalability and interoperability for decentralized applications. Validators help ensure the network runs smoothly and securely, supporting the development and deployment of various applications.
8. **Kovan**: Kovan is a test network for Ethereum that uses PoA. It allows developers to test their applications in a controlled environment before deploying them on the main network, ensuring that new applications are reliable and secure.
9. **Azure Blockchain**: Azure Blockchain, a platform by Microsoft, uses PoA to offer enterprise solutions. Validators ensure that the network is secure and efficient, making it suitable for business applications that require high reliability and performance.

Questions

1. What is a validator in the Proof of Authority (PoA) system?

    A. A creature that finds shiny pebbles

    B. A trusted participant who verifies transactions and maintains the network

    C. A friend of the Wise Old Wizard who gives out scrolls

2. Why are validators chosen in the PoA system?

    A. Because they are the fastest at solving puzzles

    B. Because of their identity and reputation

    C. Because they collect the most honey jars

3. What makes the PoA system efficient?

    A. Validators are known and trusted, so there's no need for complex calculations

    B. Validators work in a grand council chamber

    C. Validators always find the fastest way to the marketplace

4. What happens if a validator in the PoA system tries to cheat?

    A. They get a bigger reward

B. They lose their reputation and can be replaced by someone more trustworthy

  C. They become the new Wise Old Wizard

5. Which platform uses PoA to manage and track supply chains efficiently?

    A. Kovan

    B. xDai

    C. VeChain

Answers

1. **B** - A trusted participant who verifies transactions and maintains the network
2. **B** - Because of their identity and reputation
3. **A** - Validators are known and trusted, so there's no need for complex calculations
4. **B** - They lose their reputation and can be replaced by someone more trustworthy
5. **C** - VeChain

Byzantine Puzzle

A splash echoed through the forest clearing as a curious rabbit leapt into a stream, sending droplets everywhere. He emerged, holding a scroll aloft.

"Barry! You'll never guess what I found!" Robbie Rabbit called out, shaking the water off his fur.

Barry Bear looked up from his honey jars, already intrigued. "What is it now, Robbie?"

"It's from the Wise Old Wizard! He wants us to learn about Byzantine Fault Tolerance!" Robbie's eyes sparkled with excitement.

"Byzantine Fault Tolerance? That sounds interesting," Barry replied, setting aside his honey.

They made their way to the Wise Old Wizard's tower, where the Wizard greeted them warmly, his eyes twinkling with wisdom.

"Ah, Barry and Robbie, welcome," the Wizard began. "Today, we will explore the concept of Byzantine Fault Tolerance, or BFT, a system that ensures reliability and trust in our enchanted network."

Barry tilted his head. "How does BFT work?"

The Wizard nodded. "Byzantine Fault Tolerance is a system designed to reach agreement or consensus even when some participants may act maliciously or fail (consensus). It's like having a council where, despite some members being unreliable, the group can still make decisions."

Robbie's ears perked up. "So, it's like a safety net?"

"Exactly, Robbie," the Wizard replied. "BFT ensures that our network continues to function correctly, even if some parts fail or try to deceive others (fault tolerance)."

With a wave of the Wizard's staff, a shimmering portal opened, leading them into a grand hall filled with council members.

"First, let's explore the basics of BFT," the Wizard said, leading them to the council chamber. "Imagine a group of generals trying to agree on a battle plan. Some may be traitors, but the loyal ones must ensure they agree on the same plan. This is the essence of BFT (Byzantine generals problem)."

Barry watched as the council members debated and reached a decision despite some members disagreeing. "So, they find a way to agree even if some are untrustworthy?"

"Precisely, Barry," the Wizard replied. "BFT allows systems to remain reliable and reach consensus despite failures or malicious actors."

Robbie hopped around the chamber. "What happens if too many members are untrustworthy?"

The Wizard smiled. "If too many members act maliciously, the system may fail. BFT works best when the number of untrustworthy members is less than a third of the total (fault tolerance limit)."

They moved on to a bustling marketplace where creatures traded various goods. "Now, let's explore some real-world applications of BFT," the Wizard announced.

Barry saw a group of pixies managing a secure messaging platform. "What's this?"

"That's Tendermint," the Wizard explained. "Tendermint uses BFT to ensure that messages and transactions are processed reliably and securely. Validators work together to reach consensus, ensuring the system functions correctly (Tendermint)."

Robbie sniffed the air. "Smells like opportunity!"

The Wizard chuckled. "Indeed, Robbie. Another example is Hyperledger Fabric, a platform for building enterprise-level applications. It uses BFT to maintain trust and reliability in business transactions (Hyperledger Fabric)."

Next, they arrived at a serene garden where creatures collaborated on projects. "This is Cosmos," the Wizard said. "Cosmos uses BFT to connect multiple blockchains, allowing them to interact and exchange information securely (Cosmos)."

Barry's eyes widened. "That's incredible! What else?"

The Wizard led them to a bustling workshop where creatures crafted unique items. "This is Ripple," the Wizard explained. "Ripple uses BFT to enable fast and secure cross-border payments. Validators ensure that transactions are processed quickly and accurately (Ripple)."

Robbie clapped his paws. "This place is amazing! Anything else?"

The Wizard nodded. "There's also Zilliqa, a high-throughput blockchain platform that uses BFT to ensure scalability and security for decentralized applications (Zilliqa)."

Barry and Robbie spent the rest of the day exploring the world of BFT, amazed by its reliability and the innovative projects built within it. By the time the sun began to set, they felt enlightened and excited about the endless possibilities.

As they made their way back through the portal, Robbie couldn't help but make Barry laugh with his impressions of the Wise Old Wizard explaining BFT's wonders.

Barry, feeling wiser and more connected, knew that with the power of BFT, they could explore and innovate in ways they had never imagined.

Explanation of Concepts

1. **Consensus**: Byzantine Fault Tolerance (BFT) is a system designed to reach agreement or consensus even when some participants may act maliciously or fail. It ensures that a network can make decisions and remain functional despite the presence of untrustworthy members.
2. **Fault Tolerance**: BFT ensures that a network continues to function correctly even if some parts fail or try to deceive others. It provides a safety net that maintains reliability and trust within the system.
3. **Byzantine Generals Problem**: This is a thought experiment that illustrates the challenges of reaching consensus in a network with unreliable members. BFT solves this problem by ensuring that loyal participants can agree on a decision despite the presence of traitors.
4. **Fault Tolerance Limit**: BFT works best when the number of untrustworthy members is less than a third of the total participants. If too many members act maliciously, the system may fail, but within the fault tolerance limit, it remains reliable.
5. **Tendermint**: A platform that uses BFT to ensure secure and reliable processing of messages and transactions. Validators work together to reach consensus, maintaining the system's integrity.
6. **Hyperledger Fabric**: An enterprise-level platform for building applications that use BFT to maintain trust and

reliability in business transactions. It ensures that all participants can rely on the system's accuracy and security.

7. **Cosmos**: A platform that connects multiple blockchains using BFT to allow secure interaction and information exchange. It ensures that different blockchains can communicate reliably.
8. **Ripple**: A payment platform that uses BFT to enable fast and secure cross-border payments. Validators ensure that transactions are processed quickly and accurately, providing a reliable payment system.
9. **Zilliqa**: A high-throughput blockchain platform that uses BFT to ensure scalability and security for decentralized applications. It supports large-scale applications with reliable consensus and fault tolerance.

Questions

1. What does Byzantine Fault Tolerance (BFT) help a network do?

    A. Find shiny pebbles in the forest

    B. Reach agreement even if some members are untrustworthy

    C. Make honey jars disappear

2. Why is Byzantine Fault Tolerance important in a network?

    A. It ensures that the network can function correctly even if some parts fail or try to deceive others

    B. It helps the Wise Old Wizard find lost scrolls

    C. It makes the network move faster

3. What is the Byzantine Generals Problem an example of?

    A. A game played by the forest animals

    B. The challenge of reaching consensus when some members may act maliciously

    C. A puzzle that the Wise Old Wizard created

4. What happens if too many members in a Byzantine Fault Tolerance system are untrustworthy?

    A. The system becomes stronger

    B. The system may fail

C. The untrustworthy members become the leaders

5. Which platform uses BFT to ensure fast and secure cross-border payments?

   A. Cosmos

   B. Tendermint

   C. Ripple

Answers

1. **B** - Reach agreement even if some members are untrustworthy
2. **A** - It ensures that the network can function correctly even if some parts fail or try to deceive others
3. **B** - The challenge of reaching consensus when some members may act maliciously
4. **B** - The system may fail
5. **C** - Ripple

Rules Written Openly

A loud rustling erupted from the bushes as a rabbit burst through, carrying a scroll in his paw. Robbie Rabbit, with his trademark enthusiasm, hopped over to Barry Bear, nearly tripping over his own feet in excitement.

"Barry! You've got to see this! The Wise Old Wizard has sent us a new quest!" Robbie exclaimed.

Barry looked up from his honey jars, intrigued. "What's it about this time, Robbie?"

"It's about on-chain governance! The Wizard wants us to learn how it works and why it's important!" Robbie said, eyes twinkling with curiosity.

"On-chain governance? That sounds intriguing," Barry replied, already interested.

They made their way to the Wise Old Wizard's tower, where the Wizard greeted them warmly, his eyes sparkling with knowledge.

"Ah, Barry and Robbie, welcome," the Wizard began. "Today, we will explore the concept of on-chain governance, a system that allows the community to make decisions directly within our enchanted network."

Barry tilted his head. "How does on-chain governance work?"

The Wizard nodded. "On-chain governance is a system where decisions about the network are made through votes directly recorded on the network itself (voting on the blockchain). It's like having a town council where everyone's vote is counted and recorded transparently."

Robbie's ears perked up. "So, everyone gets a say?"

"Exactly, Robbie," the Wizard replied. "This system ensures that all participants can have a voice in the decision-making process, making it more democratic and transparent (participatory democracy)."

With a wave of the Wizard's staff, a shimmering portal opened, leading them into a grand hall filled with council members.

"First, let's explore how proposals are made and voted on," the Wizard said, leading them to the council chamber. "Anyone in the community can propose changes or new rules. These proposals are then voted on by the community, and if they receive enough support, they are implemented (proposal and voting process)."

Barry watched as a squirrel proposed a new rule and the community voted on it. "So, it's all done openly and everyone can see the results?"

"Precisely, Barry," the Wizard replied. "This transparency ensures that decisions are made fairly and that everyone can trust the process."

Robbie hopped around the chamber. "What happens if someone tries to manipulate the vote?"

The Wizard smiled. "The system is designed to prevent manipulation by requiring that changes are supported by a significant portion of the community. This makes it difficult for any one individual or group to control the outcome (security and fairness)."

They moved on to a bustling marketplace where creatures traded various goods. "Now, let's explore some real-world applications of on-chain governance," the Wizard announced.

Barry saw a group of pixies managing a decentralized trading platform. "What's this?"

"That's Tezos," the Wizard explained. "Tezos uses on-chain governance to allow its community to vote on protocol upgrades. This ensures that the network can evolve and improve over time based on the collective input of its users (Tezos)."

Robbie sniffed the air. "Smells like opportunity!"

The Wizard chuckled. "Indeed, Robbie. Another example is Polkadot, a platform that uses on-chain governance to manage multiple interconnected blockchains. This allows the community to coordinate upgrades and changes across the entire ecosystem (Polkadot)."

Next, they arrived at a serene garden where creatures collaborated on projects. "This is Decred," the Wizard said. "Decred uses on-chain governance to make decisions about project funding and development. This ensures that the community can guide the direction of the project (Decred)."

Barry's eyes widened. "That's incredible! What else?"

The Wizard led them to a bustling workshop where creatures crafted unique items. "This is DAOstack," the Wizard explained. "DAOstack uses on-chain governance to manage decentralized autonomous organizations. This allows these organizations to make decisions collectively and transparently (DAOstack)."

Robbie clapped his paws. "This place is amazing! Anything else?"

The Wizard nodded. "There's also MakerDAO, a platform that uses on-chain governance to manage a decentralized stablecoin system. The community votes on changes to the system's parameters, ensuring stability and responsiveness (MakerDAO)."

Barry and Robbie spent the rest of the day exploring the world of on-chain governance, amazed by its transparency and the innovative projects built within it. By the time the sun began to set, they felt enlightened and excited about the endless possibilities.

As they made their way back through the portal, Robbie couldn't help but make Barry laugh with his impressions of the Wise Old Wizard explaining on-chain governance's wonders.

Barry, feeling wiser and more connected, knew that with the power of on-chain governance, they could explore and innovate in ways they had never imagined.

Blockchain Bedtime Stories

Explanation of Concepts

1. **Voting on the Blockchain**: On-chain governance is a system where decisions about the network are made through votes directly recorded on the network itself. It ensures that all decisions are transparent, and everyone's vote is counted.
2. **Participatory Democracy**: On-chain governance allows all participants to have a voice in the decision-making process. This makes the system more democratic and ensures that everyone can influence the direction of the network.
3. **Proposal and Voting Process**: In on-chain governance, anyone in the community can propose changes or new rules. These proposals are then voted on by the community, and if they receive enough support, they are implemented. This process ensures that decisions are made openly and transparently.
4. **Security and Fairness**: The system is designed to prevent manipulation by requiring that changes are supported by a significant portion of the community. This ensures that no single individual or group can control the outcome of the vote, maintaining fairness and security.
5. **Tezos**: Tezos uses on-chain governance to allow its community to vote on protocol upgrades. This ensures that the network can evolve and improve over time based on the collective input of its users, making it a dynamic and adaptable platform.

6. **Polkadot**: Polkadot uses on-chain governance to manage multiple interconnected blockchains. This allows the community to coordinate upgrades and changes across the entire ecosystem, enhancing cooperation and innovation.
7. **Decred**: Decred uses on-chain governance to make decisions about project funding and development. This ensures that the community can guide the direction of the project, promoting sustainable and community-driven growth.
8. **DAOstack**: DAOstack uses on-chain governance to manage decentralized autonomous organizations. This allows these organizations to make decisions collectively and transparently, fostering collaboration and efficiency.
9. **MakerDAO**: MakerDAO uses on-chain governance to manage a decentralized stablecoin system. The community votes on changes to the system's parameters, ensuring stability and responsiveness in managing the value of the stablecoin.

Questions

1. What does on-chain governance allow the community to do?

    A. Make decisions by voting directly on the network

    B. Organize honey jars

    C. Find hidden treasure in the forest

2. How is voting done in on-chain governance?

    A. By writing votes on scrolls and hiding them in the woods

    B. Through votes directly recorded on the blockchain

    C. By shouting the loudest in the council chamber

3. What is the purpose of the proposal and voting process in on-chain governance?

    A. To choose the best rabbit to lead the community

    B. To allow the community to propose changes and vote on them transparently

    C. To find the most delicious berries in the forest

4. Why is security and fairness important in on-chain governance?

    A. It helps the Wizard keep track of all the scrolls

B. It ensures that no single individual or group can control the outcome of the vote

C. It makes the voting process more fun for everyone

5. Which platform uses on-chain governance to allow its community to vote on protocol upgrades?

   A. Polkadot

   B. Tezos

   C. MakerDAO

Answers

1. **A** - Make decisions by voting directly on the network
2. **B** - Through votes directly recorded on the blockchain
3. **B** - To allow the community to propose changes and vote on them transparently
4. **B** - It ensures that no single individual or group can control the outcome of the vote
5. **B** - Tezos

Off-Chain Council

A loud rustling noise emanated from the bushes as Robbie Rabbit emerged, triumphantly holding a scroll in his paw.

"Barry! You won't believe what I've found!" Robbie Rabbit exclaimed, hopping with excitement.

Barry Bear, busy organizing his collection of honey jars, looked up curiously. "What's it this time, Robbie?"

"It's a message from the Wise Old Wizard! He wants us to learn about off-chain governance!" Robbie said, his eyes sparkling with curiosity.

"Off-chain governance? That sounds intriguing," Barry replied, setting aside his honey jar.

They made their way to the Wise Old Wizard's tower, where the Wizard greeted them warmly, his eyes twinkling with knowledge.

"Ah, Barry and Robbie, welcome," the Wizard began. "Today, we will explore the concept of off-chain governance, a system that allows decisions to be made outside our enchanted network."

Barry tilted his head. "How does off-chain governance work?"

The Wizard nodded. "Off-chain governance involves making decisions through discussions, voting, and agreements that are not recorded directly on the network (external decision-making). It's like having a town meeting where everyone can discuss and decide on matters before recording the final decisions."

Robbie's ears perked up. "So, it's like having a big discussion?"

"Exactly, Robbie," the Wizard replied. "This system allows for more flexibility and often involves key community members or developers in the decision-making process (flexible decision-making)."

With a wave of the Wizard's staff, a shimmering portal opened, leading them into a grand meeting hall filled with animated discussions.

"First, let's explore how decisions are made off-chain," the Wizard said, leading them to the center of the hall. "Here, community members and developers gather to discuss proposals. After thorough deliberation, they vote on these proposals, and the final decisions are implemented based on the consensus reached (deliberation and consensus)."

Barry watched as a fox presented a proposal and the community members debated its merits. "So, it's all about discussion and reaching an agreement?"

"Precisely, Barry," the Wizard replied. "This process allows for in-depth discussion and consideration of different viewpoints, leading to well-rounded decisions."

Robbie hopped around the hall. "What happens if they can't agree?"

The Wizard smiled. "In such cases, the community may delay the decision or continue discussions until a consensus is reached. This ensures that all voices are heard and the best possible decision is made (extended deliberation)."

They moved on to a bustling marketplace where creatures traded various goods. "Now, let's explore some real-world applications of off-chain governance," the Wizard announced.

Barry saw a group of pixies managing a decentralized trading platform. "What's this?"

"That's Bitcoin," the Wizard explained. "Bitcoin relies on off-chain governance, where decisions about protocol upgrades and changes are made through discussions and agreements among developers and stakeholders (Bitcoin)."

Robbie sniffed the air. "Smells like opportunity!"

The Wizard chuckled. "Indeed, Robbie. Another example is Ethereum Classic, a platform that uses off-chain governance to manage its development and upgrades. Key community members and developers engage in discussions to guide the platform's evolution (Ethereum Classic)."

Next, they arrived at a serene garden where creatures collaborated on projects. "This is Litecoin," the Wizard said. "Litecoin uses off-chain governance to make decisions about its protocol and features. The community discusses proposals and reaches agreements before implementing changes (Litecoin)."

Barry's eyes widened. "That's incredible! What else?"

The Wizard led them to a bustling workshop where creatures crafted unique items. "This is Dash," the Wizard explained. "Dash uses a hybrid approach with both on-chain and off-chain governance. Major decisions are often discussed off-chain before being finalized on-chain through a voting process (Dash)."

Robbie clapped his paws. "This place is amazing! Anything else?"

The Wizard nodded. "There's also Zcash, a privacy-focused platform that uses off-chain governance to manage its development and feature implementations. The community engages in discussions to ensure the platform remains secure and innovative (Zcash)."

Barry and Robbie spent the rest of the day exploring the world of off-chain governance, amazed by its flexibility and the innovative projects built within it. By the time the sun began to set, they felt enlightened and excited about the endless possibilities.

As they made their way back through the portal, Robbie couldn't help but make Barry laugh with his impressions of the Wise Old Wizard explaining off-chain governance's wonders.

Barry, feeling wiser and more connected, knew that with the power of off-chain governance, they could explore and innovate in ways they had never imagined.

Explanation of Concepts

1. **External Decision-Making**: Off-chain governance involves making decisions through discussions, voting, and agreements that are not recorded directly on the network. This allows for more flexibility in decision-making processes and the inclusion of diverse perspectives.
2. **Flexible Decision-Making**: Off-chain governance allows for more flexibility and often involves key community members or developers in the decision-making process. This system enables thorough deliberation and consideration of different viewpoints, leading to well-rounded decisions.
3. **Deliberation and Consensus**: Decisions in off-chain governance are made through community discussions and voting. After thorough deliberation, the final decisions are implemented based on the consensus reached among participants.
4. **Extended Deliberation**: If consensus cannot be reached immediately, the community may delay the decision or continue discussions until a consensus is achieved. This ensures that all voices are heard and the best possible decision is made.
5. **Bitcoin**: Bitcoin relies on off-chain governance, where decisions about protocol upgrades and changes are made through discussions and agreements among developers and stakeholders. This process ensures that the network remains secure and efficient.

6. **Ethereum Classic**: A platform that uses off-chain governance to manage its development and upgrades. Key community members and developers engage in discussions to guide the platform's evolution, ensuring its continuous improvement.
7. **Litecoin**: Litecoin uses off-chain governance to make decisions about its protocol and features. The community discusses proposals and reaches agreements before implementing changes, maintaining a collaborative and flexible approach.
8. **Dash**: Dash uses a hybrid approach with both on-chain and off-chain governance. Major decisions are often discussed off-chain before being finalized on-chain through a voting process, combining the benefits of both systems.
9. **Zcash**: A privacy-focused platform that uses off-chain governance to manage its development and feature implementations. The community engages in discussions to ensure the platform remains secure and innovative, fostering continuous improvement.

Questions

1. What is off-chain governance?

    A. A system where decisions are made outside the network through discussions and agreements

    B. A method of organizing honey jars

    C. A way to find hidden treasure in the forest

2. How are decisions made in off-chain governance?

    A. By rolling dice

    B. Through community discussions, voting, and reaching agreements

    C. By asking the Wise Old Wizard directly

3. What happens if the community cannot agree on a decision in off-chain governance?

    A. The decision is made by the Wizard alone

    B. The community delays the decision or continues discussions until consensus is reached

    C. They cancel the meeting and go home

4. Which platform uses off-chain governance to make decisions about its protocol upgrades?

    A. Litecoin

    B. Bitcoin

    C. Zcash

5. What type of governance approach does Dash use?

    A. Only off-chain governance

    B. Only on-chain governance

    C. A hybrid approach with both on-chain and off-chain governance

Answers

1. **A** - A system where decisions are made outside the network through discussions and agreements
2. **B** - Through community discussions, voting, and reaching agreements
3. **B** - The community delays the decision or continues discussions until consensus is reached
4. **B** - Bitcoin
5. **C** - A hybrid approach with both on-chain and off-chain governance

Cross-Chain Conundrum

A colorful feather floated down from the treetops, landing right at the feet of a bustling rabbit. Robbie Rabbit, eyes bright with curiosity, snatched up the feather and waved it in front of Barry Bear.

"Barry! Look at this! A message from the Wise Old Wizard!" Robbie exclaimed, hopping in excitement.

Barry Bear, engrossed in organizing his collection of shiny pebbles, turned his attention to Robbie. "What does it say?"

"It's about something called interoperability! The Wizard wants us to learn why it's important and how it works!" Robbie said, eyes gleaming with curiosity.

"Interoperability? That sounds intriguing," Barry replied, already interested.

They made their way to the Wise Old Wizard's tower, where the Wizard greeted them warmly, his eyes sparkling with wisdom.

"Ah, Barry and Robbie, welcome," the Wizard began. "Today, we will explore the concept of interoperability, a crucial aspect of our interconnected network."

Barry tilted his head. "How does interoperability work?"

The Wizard nodded. "Interoperability refers to the ability of different systems to communicate and work together seamlessly (cross-chain communication). It's like different villages being able to trade and share resources efficiently."

Robbie's ears perked up. "So, it's about making sure everyone can work together?"

"Exactly, Robbie," the Wizard replied. "This system ensures that different networks can exchange information and value without barriers, making the whole ecosystem more powerful and cohesive (network integration)."

With a wave of the Wizard's staff, a shimmering portal opened, leading them into a grand marketplace bustling with activity.

"First, let's explore the importance of cross-chain communication," the Wizard said, leading them to the center of the marketplace. "Imagine each stall here represents a different village. Without interoperability, these villages can't trade with each other, limiting their growth and potential (isolation)."

Barry watched as a fox struggled to trade with a rabbit from another village due to the lack of a common system. "So, they need a way to communicate and trade?"

"Precisely, Barry," the Wizard replied. "Interoperability allows these different villages to connect, share resources, and grow together. This creates a more vibrant and efficient marketplace (enhanced cooperation)."

Robbie hopped around the marketplace. "What happens if they can't communicate properly?"

The Wizard smiled. "If they can't communicate, they remain isolated and miss out on opportunities for growth and collaboration. Interoperability solves this by creating bridges between different systems, allowing them to work together (bridging systems)."

They moved on to a bustling trade fair where creatures showcased their unique goods. "Now, let's explore some real-world applications of interoperability," the Wizard announced.

Barry saw a group of pixies managing a platform that connected various trading systems. "What's this?"

"That's Polkadot," the Wizard explained. "Polkadot uses interoperability to connect multiple blockchains, allowing them to communicate and share information. This enables different networks to work together efficiently (Polkadot)."

Robbie sniffed the air. "Smells like opportunity!"

The Wizard chuckled. "Indeed, Robbie. Another example is Cosmos, a platform designed to enable interoperability between different blockchains. It uses a system of hubs and zones to facilitate communication and value exchange (Cosmos)."

Next, they arrived at a serene garden where creatures collaborated on projects. "This is Aion," the Wizard said. "Aion focuses on creating bridges between different blockchains, allowing them to communicate and share resources effectively (Aion)."

Barry's eyes widened. "That's incredible! What else?"

The Wizard led them to a bustling port where creatures exchanged various assets. "This is Wanchain," the Wizard explained. "Wanchain uses interoperability to connect different blockchain networks, enabling seamless transfer of assets and information (Wanchain)."

Robbie clapped his paws. "This place is amazing! Anything else?"

The Wizard nodded. "There's also Ark, which focuses on creating a web of connected blockchains. Ark's system allows for easy integration and communication between different networks, enhancing their collective capabilities (Ark)."

Barry and Robbie spent the rest of the day exploring the world of interoperability, amazed by its ability to connect diverse systems and the innovative projects built within it. By the time the sun began to set, they felt enlightened and excited about the endless possibilities.

As they made their way back through the portal, Robbie couldn't help but make Barry laugh with his impressions of the Wise Old Wizard explaining interoperability's wonders.

Barry, feeling wiser and more connected, knew that with the power of interoperability, they could explore and innovate in ways they had never imagined.

Explanation of Concepts

1. **Cross-Chain Communication**: Interoperability refers to the ability of different systems or networks to communicate and work together seamlessly. It ensures that different networks can exchange information and value without barriers, creating a more cohesive ecosystem.
2. **Network Integration**: This system ensures that different networks can connect, share resources, and grow together. By integrating various networks, interoperability enhances the overall functionality and efficiency of the ecosystem.
3. **Isolation**: Without interoperability, different networks remain isolated, unable to trade or share resources. This limits their growth and potential, preventing them from benefiting from collaboration and resource sharing.
4. **Enhanced Cooperation**: Interoperability allows different systems to connect and work together, creating a more vibrant and efficient marketplace. It fosters cooperation and resource sharing, enabling networks to grow and innovate collectively.
5. **Bridging Systems**: Interoperability creates bridges between different systems, allowing them to communicate and work together. This connectivity enables seamless interaction and collaboration between diverse networks.

6. **Polkadot**: A platform that uses interoperability to connect multiple blockchains, allowing them to communicate and share information. This enables different networks to work together efficiently and enhances their collective capabilities.
7. **Cosmos**: A platform designed to enable interoperability between different blockchains. It uses a system of hubs and zones to facilitate communication and value exchange, promoting collaboration between networks.
8. **Aion**: A project focused on creating bridges between different blockchains, allowing them to communicate and share resources effectively. This enhances the connectivity and functionality of the blockchain ecosystem.
9. **Wanchain**: A platform that uses interoperability to connect different blockchain networks, enabling seamless transfer of assets and information. It promotes efficient and secure communication between diverse systems.
10. **Ark**: A project that focuses on creating a web of connected blockchains. Ark's system allows for easy integration and communication between different networks, enhancing their collective capabilities and fostering innovation.

Questions

1. What is interoperability?

    A. A system where different networks work together and communicate seamlessly

    B. A way to organize shiny pebbles

    C. A method for finding hidden treasures in the forest

2. Why is cross-chain communication important?

    A. It helps creatures find more food in the forest

    B. It allows different networks to share information and resources without barriers

    C. It makes the forest quieter at night

3. What happens if different networks cannot communicate properly?

    A. They become stronger and grow faster

    B. They remain isolated and miss out on opportunities for growth and collaboration

    C. They merge into one big network

4. Which platform uses interoperability to connect multiple blockchains, allowing them to share information?

A. Cosmos

   B. Polkadot

   C. Wanchain

5. What does the Ark platform focus on?

   A. Organizing trade fairs in the forest

   B. Creating a web of connected blockchains for easy integration and communication

   C. Growing the biggest and tastiest berries

Answers

1. **A** - A system where different networks work together and communicate seamlessly
2. **B** - It allows different networks to share information and resources without barriers
3. **B** - They remain isolated and miss out on opportunities for growth and collaboration
4. **B** - Polkadot
5. **B** - Creating a web of connected blockchains for easy integration and communication

Protocols of Connectivity

A brilliant sunbeam pierced through the forest canopy, catching the glint of a curious rabbit's eyes. Robbie Rabbit, ever the enthusiastic explorer, darted over to Barry Bear, holding a scroll aloft.

"Barry! You won't believe what I've got here!" Robbie exclaimed, practically vibrating with excitement.

Barry looked up from his honey jars, curiosity piqued. "What is it this time, Robbie?"

"It's from the Wise Old Wizard! He wants us to learn about protocols for interoperability!" Robbie said, eyes twinkling.

"Interoperability? That sounds intriguing," Barry replied, already interested.

They made their way to the Wise Old Wizard's tower, where the Wizard greeted them warmly, his eyes sparkling with wisdom.

"Ah, Barry and Robbie, welcome," the Wizard began. "Today, we will explore the concept of interoperability protocols, focusing on Cosmos and Polkadot, and a few other emerging protocols."

Barry tilted his head. "How do these protocols work?"

The Wizard nodded. "Interoperability protocols are systems that allow different networks to communicate and share information seamlessly (cross-chain communication). They are like bridges connecting different islands, allowing free movement of resources and information."

Robbie's ears perked up. "So, they help everyone work together?"

"Exactly, Robbie," the Wizard replied. "These protocols ensure that different networks can exchange data and value efficiently, making the entire ecosystem more cohesive and powerful (network integration)."

With a wave of the Wizard's staff, a shimmering portal opened, leading them into a grand hall filled with bustling activity.

"First, let's explore Cosmos," the Wizard said, leading them to a vibrant market. "Cosmos is designed to enable interoperability between different blockchains. It uses a system of hubs and zones to facilitate communication and value exchange (hubs and zones)."

Barry watched as a group of traders from different islands exchanged goods effortlessly. "So, Cosmos connects everyone through these hubs?"

"Precisely, Barry," the Wizard replied. "The main hub, called the Cosmos Hub, connects various zones, which are independent blockchains. This allows for seamless interaction and collaboration (Cosmos Hub)."

Robbie hopped around the market. "What about Polkadot?"

The Wizard smiled. "Polkadot is another protocol designed for interoperability. It uses a main chain called the Relay Chain to connect multiple parachains, which are individual blockchains that can communicate with each other (Relay Chain and parachains)."

They moved to another bustling section of the hall, where creatures from different lands interacted freely. "Polkadot allows these parachains to share information and assets, enabling a more integrated and efficient network (shared information)."

Barry saw a fox managing a network of connected systems. "So, they all work together seamlessly?"

"Exactly," the Wizard replied. "Polkadot's architecture ensures that different blockchains can operate in harmony, enhancing their collective capabilities."

Robbie sniffed the air. "Are there other protocols we should know about?"

The Wizard nodded. "Indeed, Robbie. Let's explore some emerging protocols."

They arrived at a serene garden where creatures collaborated on various projects. "This is Aion," the Wizard said. "Aion focuses on creating bridges between different blockchains, allowing them to communicate and share resources effectively (Aion bridges)."

Barry's eyes widened. "That's incredible! What else?"

The Wizard led them to a bustling port where creatures exchanged various assets. "This is Wanchain," the Wizard explained. "Wanchain uses interoperability to connect different blockchain networks, enabling seamless transfer of assets and information (Wanchain connectivity)."

Robbie clapped his paws. "This place is amazing! Anything else?"

The Wizard nodded. "There's also Ark, which focuses on creating a web of connected blockchains. Ark's system allows for easy integration and communication between different networks, enhancing their collective capabilities (Ark integration)."

Barry and Robbie spent the rest of the day exploring the world of interoperability protocols, amazed by their ability to connect diverse systems and the innovative projects built within them. By the time the sun began to set, they felt enlightened and excited about the endless possibilities.

As they made their way back through the portal, Robbie couldn't help but make Barry laugh with his impressions of the Wise Old Wizard explaining interoperability's wonders.

Barry, feeling wiser and more connected, knew that with the power of these protocols, they could explore and innovate in ways they had never imagined.

Explanation of Concepts

1. **Cross-Chain Communication**: Interoperability protocols enable different networks to communicate and share information seamlessly. This allows for efficient data and value exchange across diverse systems, enhancing overall network functionality.
2. **Network Integration**: These protocols create connections between various networks, ensuring they can work together effectively. This integration allows for resource sharing and collaboration, making the ecosystem more cohesive and powerful.
3. **Hubs and Zones (Cosmos)**: Cosmos uses a system of hubs and zones to facilitate communication and value exchange between different blockchains. The Cosmos Hub connects various zones, allowing for seamless interaction and collaboration.
4. **Relay Chain and Parachains (Polkadot)**: Polkadot's architecture involves a main chain called the Relay Chain, which connects multiple parachains. These parachains are individual blockchains that can communicate and share information, enabling a more integrated network.
5. **Aion Bridges**: Aion focuses on creating bridges between different blockchains, allowing them to communicate and share resources effectively. This enhances the connectivity and functionality of the blockchain ecosystem.

6. **Wanchain Connectivity**: Wanchain uses interoperability to connect different blockchain networks, enabling seamless transfer of assets and information. It promotes efficient and secure communication between diverse systems.
7. **Ark Integration**: Ark focuses on creating a web of connected blockchains. Its system allows for easy integration and communication between different networks, enhancing their collective capabilities and fostering innovation.

Questions

1. What is the main purpose of interoperability protocols, as explained by the Wise Old Wizard?

    A. To build houses for animals.

    B. To allow different networks to communicate and share information seamlessly.

    C. To make the forest bigger.

    D. To stop networks from talking to each other.

2. In the story, how does the Cosmos protocol connect different blockchains?

    A. Using bridges and tunnels.

    B. Through a system of hubs and zones.

    C. By building tall towers.

    D. With magic spells only the Wizard knows.

3. What is the main chain called in the Polkadot protocol that connects multiple parachains?

    A. The Relay Chain.

    B. The Rabbit Run.

    C. The Bear Path.

    D. The Kangaroo Jump.

4. Which protocol focuses on creating bridges between different blockchains to help them communicate and share resources?

    A. Wanchain.

    B. Ark.

    C. Aion.

    D. Cosmos.

5. What do all the protocols like Cosmos, Polkadot, Aion, Wanchain, and Ark help different networks to do?

    A. Stay separate and not share anything.

    B. Communicate and work together smoothly.

    C. Compete to see who is the best.

    D. Build fences around themselves.

Answers

1. **B** - To allow different networks to communicate and share information seamlessly.
2. **B** - Through a system of hubs and zones.
3. **A** - The Relay Chain.
4. **C** - Aion.
5. **B** - Communicate and work together smoothly.

Three Tokens of Power

A dazzling rainbow arched across the sky, casting vibrant colors on the forest below. Robbie Rabbit, with his nose twitching in excitement, bounded over to Barry Bear, waving a scroll excitedly.

"Barry! Look at this! The Wise Old Wizard has given us a new quest!" Robbie exclaimed, hopping around in circles.

Barry, engrossed in sorting his collection of shiny pebbles, looked up with a smile. "What's it about this time, Robbie?"

"It's about different types of tokens! We need to learn about utility, governance, and security tokens!" Robbie said, his eyes twinkling with curiosity.

"Different types of tokens? That sounds interesting," Barry replied, setting aside his pebbles.

They made their way to the Wise Old Wizard's tower, where the Wizard greeted them warmly, his eyes twinkling with wisdom.

"Ah, Barry and Robbie, welcome," the Wizard began. "Today, we will explore the world of tokens, focusing on utility, governance, and security tokens."

Barry tilted his head. "What are these tokens, and how do they work?"

The Wizard nodded. "Tokens are special objects that represent different kinds of value and functionality within our enchanted network (tokens). They can be used for various purposes, such as accessing services, voting on decisions, or representing ownership."

Robbie's ears perked up. "So, there are different types of tokens for different purposes?"

"Exactly, Robbie," the Wizard replied. "Let's start with utility tokens. These tokens are used to access specific services or functions within a network (utility tokens). They are like magical keys that unlock certain features."

With a wave of the Wizard's staff, a shimmering portal opened, leading them into a bustling marketplace filled with activity.

"First, let's explore how utility tokens work," the Wizard said, leading them to a stand where a fox was trading tokens for enchanted items. "Utility tokens give you access to specific services or features, like purchasing items or using special abilities."

Barry watched as the fox used a token to unlock a hidden treasure chest. "So, these tokens can be used like money to get things?"

"Precisely, Barry," the Wizard replied. "They are essential for accessing various functions within the network."

Robbie hopped around the marketplace. "What about governance tokens?"

The Wizard smiled. "Governance tokens allow holders to vote on important decisions about how the network operates (governance tokens). They give the community a voice in shaping the future of the network."

They moved on to a grand council chamber where creatures were voting on different proposals. "Governance tokens give you the power to influence decisions, such as changes to rules or new features," the Wizard explained.

Barry saw a squirrel voting on a proposal to plant more magical trees. "So, it's like having a say in how things are run?"

"Exactly," the Wizard replied. "Governance tokens ensure that the community can participate in decision-making."

Robbie sniffed the air. "And what about security tokens?"

The Wizard nodded. "Security tokens represent ownership or investment in an asset, like shares in a company (security tokens). They are like enchanted certificates that prove you own something valuable."

They arrived at a grand castle where creatures traded tokens representing shares in various ventures. "Security tokens can represent ownership in projects or assets, and they often come with rights such as dividends or profit sharing," the Wizard explained.

Barry watched as a pixie traded tokens for a share in a new magical invention. "So, these tokens are like owning a piece of something valuable?"

"Precisely," the Wizard replied. "Security tokens provide a way to invest and share in the success of different ventures."

Robbie clapped his paws. "This place is amazing! Anything else?"

The Wizard nodded. "There are also emerging types of tokens, but utility, governance, and security tokens are the most common and important ones. They each play a unique role in our enchanted network."

Barry and Robbie spent the rest of the day exploring the world of tokens, amazed by their versatility and the innovative projects built within them. By the time the sun began to set, they felt enlightened and excited about the endless possibilities.

As they made their way back through the portal, Robbie couldn't help but make Barry laugh with his impressions of the Wise Old Wizard explaining the different types of tokens.

Barry, feeling wiser and more connected, knew that with the power of these tokens, they could explore and innovate in ways they had never imagined.

Explanation of Concepts

1. **Tokens**: Special objects that represent different kinds of value and functionality within a network. Tokens can be used for various purposes, such as accessing services, voting on decisions, or representing ownership in assets.
2. **Utility Tokens**: Tokens used to access specific services or functions within a network. They act like magical keys that unlock certain features, allowing users to purchase items or use special abilities.
3. **Governance Tokens**: Tokens that allow holders to vote on important decisions about how the network operates. They give the community a voice in shaping the future of the network, enabling participation in decision-making processes.
4. **Security Tokens**: Tokens that represent ownership or investment in an asset, similar to shares in a company. Security tokens prove ownership and often come with rights such as dividends or profit sharing, providing a way to invest and share in the success of ventures.
5. **Cross-Chain Communication**: Interoperability protocols enable different networks to communicate and share information seamlessly. This allows for efficient data and value exchange across diverse systems, enhancing overall network functionality.
6. **Network Integration**: These protocols create connections between various networks, ensuring they can work together effectively. This integration allows

for resource sharing and collaboration, making the ecosystem more cohesive and powerful.

7. **Hubs and Zones (Cosmos)**: Cosmos uses a system of hubs and zones to facilitate communication and value exchange between different blockchains. The Cosmos Hub connects various zones, allowing for seamless interaction and collaboration.
8. **Relay Chain and Parachains (Polkadot)**: Polkadot's architecture involves a main chain called the Relay Chain, which connects multiple parachains. These parachains are individual blockchains that can communicate and share information, enabling a more integrated network.
9. **Aion Bridges**: Aion focuses on creating bridges between different blockchains, allowing them to communicate and share resources effectively. This enhances the connectivity and functionality of the blockchain ecosystem.
10. **Wanchain Connectivity**: Wanchain uses interoperability to connect different blockchain networks, enabling seamless transfer of assets and information. It promotes efficient and secure communication between diverse systems.
11. **Ark Integration**: Ark focuses on creating a web of connected blockchains. Its system allows for easy integration and communication between different networks, enhancing their collective capabilities and fostering innovation.

Questions

1. What are tokens in the enchanted network used for?

    A. To decorate the forest

    B. To represent different kinds of value and functionality, like accessing services or voting on decisions

    C. To collect shiny pebbles

2. What is the main purpose of utility tokens?

    A. To unlock access to specific services or functions within a network

    B. To buy honey jars

    C. To decorate the Wise Old Wizard's tower

3. How do governance tokens help the community?

    A. By allowing holders to buy enchanted items

    B. By giving holders the power to vote on important decisions about how the network operates

    C. By allowing animals to run faster

4. What do security tokens represent?

    A. Ownership or investment in an asset, like shares in a company

B. Magical spells that make trees grow faster

C. A way to find hidden treasures

5. Which type of token would you use if you wanted to have a say in how a network is run?

    A. Utility token

    B. Governance token

    C. Security token

Answers

1. **B** - To represent different kinds of value and functionality, like accessing services or voting on decisions
2. **A** - To unlock access to specific services or functions within a network
3. **B** - By giving holders the power to vote on important decisions about how the network operates
4. **A** - Ownership or investment in an asset, like shares in a company
5. **B** - Governance token

Supply Side Tales

A ray of sunlight broke through the dense forest canopy, casting a golden glow on a peculiar scene. Robbie Rabbit, with a feathered hat perched jauntily on his head, was poring over a mysterious scroll. Barry Bear, drawn by Robbie's animated chatter, ambled over with a curious expression.

"Barry! You've got to see this! The Wise Old Wizard has sent us on a quest to learn about token supply models!" Robbie exclaimed, hopping in excitement.

"Token supply models? That sounds intriguing," Barry replied, already interested.

They made their way to the Wise Old Wizard's tower, where the Wizard greeted them warmly, his eyes twinkling with knowledge.

"Ah, Barry and Robbie, welcome," the Wizard began. "Today, we will explore the concept of token supply models, specifically deflationary and inflationary models."

Barry tilted his head. "What are these supply models, and how do they work?"

The Wizard nodded. "Token supply models determine how the number of tokens in a network changes over time. Deflationary models reduce the supply, while inflationary models increase it (token supply models)."

Robbie's ears perked up. "So, there are different ways to manage how many tokens exist?"

"Exactly, Robbie," the Wizard replied. "Let's start with deflationary models. In a deflationary model, the total number of tokens decreases over time (deflationary model). It's like having a limited supply of honey jars that gradually become fewer."

With a wave of the Wizard's staff, a shimmering portal opened, leading them into a grand vault filled with glowing tokens.

"First, let's explore how deflationary models work," the Wizard said, leading them to a vault door that slowly closed. "In deflationary models, tokens are often 'burned' or removed from circulation, which increases their scarcity and potentially their value."

Barry watched as a fox deposited tokens into a magical fire, causing them to vanish. "So, fewer tokens make each one more valuable?"

"Precisely, Barry," the Wizard replied. "As the supply decreases, the value of each remaining token can increase, assuming demand stays the same or grows."

Robbie hopped around the vault. "What about inflationary models?"

The Wizard smiled. "Inflationary models work the opposite way. They increase the total number of tokens over time (inflationary model). It's like having an ever-growing supply of honey jars."

They moved to another chamber where tokens were being minted from a magical fountain. "In inflationary models, new tokens are created at a steady rate, which can help support network growth and reward participants," the Wizard explained.

Barry saw a pixie collecting freshly minted tokens from the fountain. "So, more tokens are made to keep up with growth?"

"Exactly," the Wizard replied. "This can help incentivize users and maintain the network's health, but it can also dilute the value of each token if not managed properly."

Robbie sniffed the air. "Are there examples of these models?"

The Wizard nodded. "Indeed, Robbie. Let's explore some real-world applications."

They arrived at a bustling marketplace where creatures traded various goods. "Bitcoin is a well-known example of a deflationary model," the Wizard said. "Its supply is capped at 21 million tokens, and tokens are gradually 'burned' or lost over time, increasing their scarcity (Bitcoin)."

Barry watched as a fox traded rare tokens. "So, Bitcoin becomes more valuable because there will never be more than a set amount?"

"Precisely," the Wizard replied. "Now, let's look at Ethereum, which uses an inflationary model. New tokens are continually created to reward participants and support network operations (Ethereum)."

Robbie clapped his paws. "This place is amazing! Anything else?"

The Wizard nodded. "There are also hybrid models, like Binance Coin, which starts as an inflationary model but periodically burns tokens to reduce supply, creating a balance between growth and scarcity (Binance Coin)."

Barry and Robbie spent the rest of the day exploring the world of token supply models, amazed by their complexity and the innovative projects built within them. By the time the sun began to set, they felt enlightened and excited about the endless possibilities.

As they made their way back through the portal, Robbie couldn't help but make Barry laugh with his impressions of the Wise Old Wizard explaining token supply models' wonders.

Barry, feeling wiser and more connected, knew that with the knowledge of these models, they could explore and innovate in ways they had never imagined.

Explanation of Concepts

1. **Token Supply Models**: These models determine how the number of tokens in a network changes over time. Deflationary models reduce the total supply, while inflationary models increase it. These models are crucial for understanding how token value and network health are managed.
2. **Deflationary Model**: In a deflationary model, the total number of tokens decreases over time. This is achieved by 'burning' or removing tokens from circulation. As the supply decreases, the scarcity can increase the value of each remaining token.
3. **Inflationary Model**: Inflationary models increase the total number of tokens over time. New tokens are created at a steady rate to support network growth and reward participants. However, this can dilute the value of each token if not managed properly.
4. **Bitcoin (Deflationary)**: Bitcoin is a well-known example of a deflationary model. Its supply is capped at 21 million tokens, and tokens are gradually 'burned' or lost over time, increasing their scarcity and potentially their value.
5. **Ethereum (Inflationary)**: Ethereum uses an inflationary model where new tokens are continually created to reward participants and support network operations. This helps maintain network health and incentivize users, but can dilute token value if not balanced.

6. **Binance Coin (Hybrid)**: Binance Coin uses a hybrid model, starting with an inflationary approach but periodically burning tokens to reduce supply. This creates a balance between growth and scarcity, supporting network health while managing token value.

Questions

1. What is a token supply model?

    A. A plan for how many tokens exist in a network and how that number changes over time

    B. A map showing where tokens are hidden in the forest

    C. A recipe for making tokens

2. What happens to the total number of tokens in a deflationary model?

    A. The number of tokens increases over time

    B. The number of tokens stays the same

    C. The number of tokens decreases over time

3. How does an inflationary model affect the number of tokens in a network?

    A. It decreases the number of tokens

    B. It increases the number of tokens

    C. It freezes the number of tokens

4. Which cryptocurrency is an example of a deflationary model?

    A. Bitcoin

B. Ethereum

C. Binance Coin

5. What is unique about Binance Coin's token supply model?

    A. It only decreases the number of tokens over time

    B. It combines both inflationary and deflationary models by creating new tokens and then periodically burning some of them

    C. It never changes the number of tokens

Answers

1. **A** - A plan for how many tokens exist in a network and how that number changes over time
2. **C** - The number of tokens decreases over time
3. **B** - It increases the number of tokens
4. **A** - Bitcoin
5. **B** - It combines both inflationary and deflationary models by creating new tokens and then periodically burning some of them

Scarcity Sparks Value

A dazzling ray of sunlight broke through the canopy, casting a golden glow on a peculiar scene. Robbie Rabbit, sporting a feathered hat, pored over a mysterious scroll. Barry Bear, drawn by Robbie's animated chatter, ambled over with a curious expression.

"Barry! You've got to see this! The Wise Old Wizard has sent us on a quest to learn about tokenomics!" Robbie exclaimed, hopping in excitement.

"Tokenomics? That sounds intriguing," Barry replied, already interested.

They made their way to the Wise Old Wizard's tower, where the Wizard greeted them warmly, his eyes twinkling with knowledge.

"Ah, Barry and Robbie, welcome," the Wizard began. "Today, we will explore the concept of tokenomics and its impact on our enchanted network through various case studies and examples."

Barry tilted his head. "What is tokenomics, and how does it work?"

The Wizard nodded. "Tokenomics refers to the economic principles and models governing the creation, distribution, and value of tokens within a network (economic principles).

It's like the rules that determine how our enchanted marketplace operates."

Robbie's ears perked up. "So, different tokens have different rules?"

"Exactly, Robbie," the Wizard replied. "Let's start with a case study of Bitcoin. Bitcoin's tokenomics is based on a deflationary model, where the total supply is capped at 21 million tokens (Bitcoin). This scarcity drives demand and value."

With a wave of the Wizard's staff, a shimmering portal opened, leading them into a bustling marketplace filled with traders.

"First, let's explore Bitcoin's impact," the Wizard said, leading them to a stall where a fox was trading Bitcoin tokens. "Bitcoin's fixed supply has created a sense of digital gold, where scarcity drives value and demand (digital gold)."

Barry watched as the fox traded Bitcoin for enchanted goods. "So, fewer tokens make each one more valuable?"

"Precisely, Barry," the Wizard replied. "Now, let's look at Ethereum, which uses a different model. Ethereum has a continuous issuance of new tokens to support network operations and development (Ethereum)."

Robbie hopped around the marketplace. "What's the impact of that?"

The Wizard smiled. "Ethereum's tokenomics incentivizes participation and development within the network, ensuring it remains vibrant and evolving. However, it also requires careful management to prevent inflation (network incentives)."

They moved on to a grand hall where creatures were voting on various proposals. "Next, let's examine the impact of governance tokens," the Wizard announced.

Barry saw a squirrel voting on a proposal using governance tokens. "What's this about?"

"Governance tokens allow holders to vote on important decisions about how the network operates," the Wizard explained. "This creates a sense of community ownership and engagement (governance)."

Robbie sniffed the air. "Are there other examples?"

The Wizard nodded. "Indeed, Robbie. Let's explore Binance Coin (BNB), which uses a hybrid model. Binance Coin started with an inflationary model but periodically burns tokens to reduce supply and increase value (hybrid model)."

They arrived at a serene garden where creatures traded various assets. "BNB's tokenomics has created a dynamic ecosystem where token burning helps manage supply and maintain value (token burning)."

Barry watched as a pixie traded BNB tokens for enchanted items. "So, burning tokens makes them scarcer and more valuable?"

"Exactly," the Wizard replied. "Now, let's look at DeFi projects like Uniswap, which use utility tokens to incentivize liquidity provision and trading (DeFi)."

Robbie clapped his paws. "This place is amazing! How do these utility tokens work?"

"Utility tokens give holders access to specific services or functions within the network," the Wizard explained. "In Uniswap's case, utility tokens reward users for providing liquidity, ensuring the market remains active and efficient (liquidity incentives)."

Barry and Robbie spent the rest of the day exploring the world of tokenomics, amazed by the different models and their impacts on the network. By the time the sun began to set, they felt enlightened and excited about the endless possibilities.

As they made their way back through the portal, Robbie couldn't help but make Barry laugh with his impressions of the Wise Old Wizard explaining the wonders of tokenomics.

Barry, feeling wiser and more connected, knew that with the knowledge of these tokenomics models, they could explore and innovate in ways they had never imagined.

Explanation of Concepts

1. **Economic Principles (Tokenomics)**: Tokenomics refers to the economic principles and models governing the creation, distribution, and value of tokens within a network. It determines how tokens are issued, how their supply is managed, and how they gain value.
2. **Bitcoin**: Bitcoin's tokenomics is based on a deflationary model, where the total supply is capped at 21 million tokens. This scarcity drives demand and value, making Bitcoin often referred to as digital gold due to its limited supply.
3. **Digital Gold**: Bitcoin is often compared to gold because of its limited supply and increasing value over time. The fixed supply and deflationary nature create a sense of scarcity, driving demand and value.
4. **Ethereum**: Ethereum's tokenomics involves continuous issuance of new tokens to support network operations and development. This model incentivizes participation and development within the network but requires careful management to prevent inflation.
5. **Network Incentives**: Ethereum's continuous issuance of new tokens incentivizes users to participate in and develop the network. This helps ensure the network remains active and evolves over time but must be balanced to avoid devaluing the tokens.
6. **Governance Tokens**: Governance tokens allow holders to vote on important decisions about how the network operates. This creates a sense of community

ownership and engagement, as token holders have a direct influence on the network's direction.

7. **Hybrid Model (Binance Coin)**: Binance Coin (BNB) uses a hybrid tokenomics model that started with an inflationary approach but periodically burns tokens to reduce supply. This helps manage the token's value by creating scarcity over time.
8. **Token Burning**: Token burning involves permanently removing tokens from circulation, reducing the total supply. This process can help increase the value of remaining tokens by creating scarcity, as seen with Binance Coin's tokenomics.
9. **DeFi (Decentralized Finance)**: DeFi projects like Uniswap use utility tokens to incentivize liquidity provision and trading. These tokens reward users for contributing to the market, ensuring it remains active and efficient.
10. **Liquidity Incentives**: In DeFi projects, utility tokens are used to incentivize users to provide liquidity. This keeps the market active by ensuring there are enough tokens available for trading, which helps maintain efficiency and stability in the market.

Questions

1. What does tokenomics refer to?

    A. The rules for how tokens are hidden in the forest

    B. The economic principles governing the creation, distribution, and value of tokens within a network

    C. The magic spells used to create tokens

2. What is the impact of Bitcoin's deflationary tokenomics model?

    A. The number of Bitcoin tokens increases every year

    B. Bitcoin's fixed supply creates scarcity, which can drive up demand and value

    C. Bitcoin tokens can be created infinitely

3. How does Ethereum's tokenomics model differ from Bitcoin's?

    A. Ethereum has a fixed supply like Bitcoin

    B. Ethereum continually issues new tokens to support network operations and development

    C. Ethereum burns tokens to decrease supply

4. What is the purpose of governance tokens in a network?

    A. To allow holders to buy enchanted items

B. To allow holders to vote on important decisions about how the network operates

C. To magically increase in value without any changes in supply

5. What is the function of token burning in Binance Coin's hybrid model?

A. To increase the number of tokens available for trading

B. To permanently remove tokens from circulation, reducing the total supply and potentially increasing value

C. To make the tokens glow brighter

Answers

1. **B** - The economic principles governing the creation, distribution, and value of tokens within a network
2. **B** - Bitcoin's fixed supply creates scarcity, which can drive up demand and value
3. **B** - Ethereum continually issues new tokens to support network operations and development
4. **B** - To allow holders to vote on important decisions about how the network operates
5. **B** - To permanently remove tokens from circulation, reducing the total supply and potentially increasing value

Unveiling the Network's Hidden Dangers

A loud clatter echoed through the forest clearing as a curious rabbit tumbled out of a hollow log, clutching an ancient scroll. Robbie Rabbit, ever the eager explorer, darted over to Barry Bear, waving the scroll excitedly.

"Barry! Look what I found! The Wise Old Wizard has sent us on a quest to learn about common security threats!" Robbie exclaimed, hopping up and down.

Barry Bear, engrossed in arranging his honey jars, looked up with a smile. "Common security threats? That sounds important and intriguing."

They made their way to the Wise Old Wizard's tower, where the Wizard greeted them warmly, his eyes sparkling with wisdom.

"Ah, Barry and Robbie, welcome," the Wizard began. "Today, we will explore the world of security threats in our enchanted network, focusing on three major types: 51% attacks, double-spending, and Sybil attacks."

Barry tilted his head. "What are these threats, and how do they work?"

The Wizard nodded. "These threats are dangers that can compromise the integrity and security of our network. Let's start with the 51% attack. This occurs when a single entity gains control over more than half of the network's processing power, allowing them to manipulate transactions (51% attack)."

Robbie's ears perked up. "So, one bad actor can control everything?"

"Exactly, Robbie," the Wizard replied. "If they control over 50% of the network, they can potentially reverse transactions and double-spend tokens (double-spending)."

With a wave of the Wizard's staff, a shimmering portal opened, leading them into a grand hall filled with activity.

"First, let's explore the 51% attack," the Wizard said, leading them to a chamber where a fox controlled a majority of the network's nodes. "This fox can now manipulate transactions and undermine the network's trust."

Barry watched as the fox reversed a transaction and double-spent tokens. "So, this can really harm the network?"

"Precisely, Barry," the Wizard replied. "It disrupts the trust and reliability of the system."

Robbie hopped around the chamber. "What about double-spending?"

The Wizard smiled. "Double-spending occurs when someone spends the same token more than once by manipulating the network (double-spending). It's like using the same gold coin to buy two different items, which should be impossible."

They moved on to a bustling marketplace where creatures traded various goods. "Double-spending undermines the value of the tokens and the trust in the network," the Wizard explained.

Barry saw a fox spending the same token twice to buy different items. "So, it's like cheating?"

"Exactly," the Wizard replied. "Now, let's look at Sybil attacks. This happens when an attacker creates multiple fake identities to gain influence over the network (Sybil attack)."

They arrived at a grand council chamber where a single creature, using many identities, tried to influence decisions. "By creating numerous fake identities, the attacker can manipulate votes and decisions," the Wizard explained.

Robbie clapped his paws. "That sounds tricky! How do we stop it?"

The Wizard nodded. "To protect against these threats, we use various security measures like requiring proof of work or stake, and implementing identity verification systems (security measures)."

Barry and Robbie spent the rest of the day exploring the different security threats and the measures in place to protect against them. By the time the sun began to set, they felt enlightened and aware of the dangers and the importance of security in their network.

As they made their way back through the portal, Robbie couldn't help but make Barry laugh with his impressions of the Wise Old Wizard explaining the various threats.

Barry, feeling wiser and more vigilant, knew that with the knowledge of these threats and how to counter them, they could keep their network safe and secure.

Explanation of Concepts

1. **51% Attack**: A security threat that occurs when a single entity gains control over more than half of the network's processing power, allowing them to manipulate transactions. This can undermine the trust and reliability of the network by enabling the attacker to reverse transactions and double-spend tokens.
2. **Double-Spending**: This threat occurs when someone spends the same token more than once by manipulating the network. It undermines the value of the tokens and the trust in the network, similar to using the same gold coin to buy two different items, which should be impossible.
3. **Sybil Attack**: A security threat where an attacker creates multiple fake identities to gain influence over the network. By creating numerous fake identities, the attacker can manipulate votes and decisions, compromising the integrity of the network.
4. **Security Measures**: To protect against these threats, networks use various security measures like requiring proof of work or stake and implementing identity verification systems. These measures help ensure the integrity and trustworthiness of the network.
5. **Network Integrity**: The overall reliability and trust in the network. Maintaining network integrity involves protecting against threats like 51% attacks, double-spending, and Sybil attacks, ensuring that transactions are secure and trustworthy.

6. **Proof of Work/Stake**: Methods used to secure the network. Proof of Work requires participants to perform computational work, while Proof of Stake involves participants staking their tokens as collateral. Both methods help prevent attacks and ensure network integrity.
7. **Identity Verification Systems**: Systems that verify the identities of participants in the network. These systems help prevent Sybil attacks by ensuring that each identity is unique and trustworthy, maintaining the integrity of the network.

Questions

1. What is a 51% attack?

    A. When a rabbit finds 51% of the carrots in the forest

    B. When a single entity gains control over more than half of the network's processing power and can manipulate transactions

    C. When the Wise Old Wizard controls 51% of the network's decisions

2. What does double-spending mean?

    A. Spending the same token more than once by manipulating the network

    B. Spending twice as much money to buy the same item

    C. Spending tokens to buy double the amount of goods

3. What is a Sybil attack?

    A. When an attacker creates multiple fake identities to gain influence over the network

    B. When a fox steals tokens from others

    C. When a bear votes twice on the same proposal

4. How can networks protect against security threats like 51% attacks and Sybil attacks?

   A. By planting more magical trees

   B. By using security measures like requiring proof of work or stake and implementing identity verification systems

   C. By having the Wise Old Wizard watch over everything

5. Why is it important to maintain network integrity?

   A. To make sure all the tokens glow brightly

   B. To ensure that transactions are secure and trustworthy, and to protect against threats like 51% attacks, double-spending, and Sybil attacks

   C. To ensure that everyone gets an equal amount of honey

Answers

1. **B** - When a single entity gains control over more than half of the network's processing power and can manipulate transactions

2. **A** - Spending the same token more than once by manipulating the network
3. **A** - When an attacker creates multiple fake identities to gain influence over the network
4. **B** - By using security measures like requiring proof of work or stake and implementing identity verification systems
5. **B** - To ensure that transactions are secure and trustworthy, and to protect against threats like 51% attacks, double-spending, and Sybil attacks

Forging the Network's Shield

The forest buzzed with the cheerful chirping of birds and the soft rustling of leaves. Without warning, a sudden clatter shattered the tranquility—a rabbit, sporting a feathered hat, had stumbled over a root, desperately clutching a scroll. Robbie Rabbit, brimming with his usual boundless energy, sprang to his feet and waved the scroll enthusiastically before Barry Bear.

"Barry! The Wise Old Wizard has sent us another quest! We need to learn about best practices for security in our enchanted network!" Robbie exclaimed, his eyes shining with excitement.

"Best practices for security? That sounds essential," Barry replied, setting aside his honey jar.

They made their way to the Wise Old Wizard's tower, where the Wizard greeted them warmly, his eyes twinkling with wisdom.

"Ah, Barry and Robbie, welcome," the Wizard began. "Today, we will explore how to secure our network and smart contracts, ensuring that everything remains safe and trustworthy."

Barry tilted his head. "How do we secure the network and smart contracts?"

The Wizard nodded. "Securing our network involves multiple layers of protection. We'll start with securing the network itself. This includes using strong consensus mechanisms, regularly updating software, and monitoring for unusual activity (network security)."

Robbie's ears perked up. "So, it's like putting up strong walls and guards around our village?"

"Exactly, Robbie," the Wizard replied. "Let's start by exploring strong consensus mechanisms. These are the rules that ensure all participants agree on the state of the network (consensus mechanisms)."

With a wave of the Wizard's staff, a shimmering portal opened, leading them into a grand hall filled with bustling activity.

"First, let's explore consensus mechanisms," the Wizard said, leading them to a council chamber where creatures voted on various matters. "Strong consensus mechanisms like Proof of Work and Proof of Stake ensure that decisions are made fairly and securely (consensus mechanisms)."

Barry watched as a fox and a rabbit worked together to verify a transaction. "So, these mechanisms make sure everyone agrees and plays by the rules?"

"Precisely, Barry," the Wizard replied. "Next, we need to keep our software updated. This means regularly applying updates and patches to fix vulnerabilities and improve security (software updates)."

They moved on to a workshop where creatures were busy crafting new tools. "Regular updates help us fix any weaknesses and keep our defenses strong," the Wizard explained.

Robbie hopped around the workshop. "What about monitoring for unusual activity?"

The Wizard smiled. "Monitoring is like having watchful eyes that alert us to any suspicious behavior. This helps us catch potential threats early and respond quickly (activity monitoring)."

They arrived at a control room where a team of owls watched over the network. "By constantly monitoring the network, we can detect and address issues before they become major problems," the Wizard explained.

Barry saw an owl alerting the team to an unusual spike in activity. "So, it's like having guards who keep watch all the time?"

"Exactly," the Wizard replied. "Now, let's talk about securing smart contracts. Smart contracts are like enchanted agreements that automatically execute when conditions are met (smart contracts)."

Robbie sniffed the air. "How do we keep these agreements safe?"

The Wizard nodded. "Securing smart contracts involves several best practices. First, we must write clear and secure code to avoid vulnerabilities. This means using well-established libraries and following security guidelines (secure coding)."

They moved to a library where creatures studied ancient scrolls. "Using trusted libraries and following best practices helps us avoid common pitfalls and ensure our contracts are robust," the Wizard explained.

Barry watched as a pixie carefully coded a smart contract. "So, it's like writing clear instructions that everyone understands?"

"Precisely," the Wizard replied. "Next, we must conduct thorough testing. This involves simulating different scenarios to ensure the contract behaves as expected and doesn't have any hidden flaws (testing)."

They arrived at a testing ground where creatures ran various scenarios. "Testing helps us identify and fix issues before the contract is deployed," the Wizard explained.

Robbie clapped his paws. "This place is amazing! Anything else?"

The Wizard nodded. "Finally, we should perform regular audits. Audits involve independent reviews of our code and systems to ensure they are secure and comply with best practices (audits)."

Barry and Robbie spent the rest of the day exploring the different aspects of securing their network and smart contracts, amazed by the depth and importance of each practice. By the time the sun began to set, they felt enlightened and prepared to protect their enchanted network.

As they made their way back through the portal, Robbie couldn't help but make Barry laugh with his impressions of the Wise Old Wizard explaining security measures.

Barry, feeling wiser and more vigilant, knew that with these best practices, they could keep their network safe and secure.

Explanation of Concepts

1. **Network Security**: Securing the network involves using strong consensus mechanisms, regularly updating software, and monitoring for unusual activity. These measures help protect the network from attacks and ensure its integrity.
2. **Consensus Mechanisms**: These are rules that ensure all participants agree on the state of the network. Strong mechanisms like Proof of Work and Proof of Stake make sure decisions are made fairly and securely, preventing attacks and ensuring trust.
3. **Software Updates**: Regularly applying updates and patches to the software fixes vulnerabilities and improves security. Keeping software up-to-date helps maintain strong defenses against potential threats.
4. **Activity Monitoring**: Constantly watching the network for unusual behavior helps detect and address issues early. Monitoring acts like watchful eyes, alerting to suspicious activities and allowing quick response to potential threats.
5. **Smart Contracts**: These are automated agreements that execute when certain conditions are met. They need to be secure to ensure they function correctly and are free from vulnerabilities.
6. **Secure Coding**: Writing clear and secure code involves using well-established libraries and following security guidelines. This helps avoid common pitfalls and ensures that smart contracts are robust and reliable.

7. **Testing**: Conducting thorough testing involves simulating different scenarios to ensure the smart contract behaves as expected. Testing helps identify and fix issues before deployment, ensuring the contract's reliability.
8. **Audits**: Performing regular audits involves independent reviews of the code and systems to ensure they are secure and comply with best practices. Audits help identify potential vulnerabilities and ensure ongoing security compliance.

Questions

1. What is the purpose of network security in an enchanted network?

    A. To make the network glow brightly

    B. To protect the network from attacks and ensure its integrity by using strong consensus mechanisms, software updates, and monitoring

    C. To keep the forest animals entertained

2. What are consensus mechanisms like Proof of Work and Proof of Stake used for?

    A. To decorate the Wise Old Wizard's tower

    B. To ensure all participants agree on the state of the network and make decisions fairly and securely

    C. To make honey jars appear magically

3. Why is it important to regularly update software in a network?

    A. To make the software look new and shiny

    B. To fix vulnerabilities and improve security, keeping the network's defenses strong

    C. To make the network run faster without any purpose

4. What does activity monitoring do for a network?

   A. It helps the network grow more trees

   B. It watches for unusual behavior, alerting to potential threats so they can be addressed quickly

   C. It counts how many animals are using the network

5. Why should smart contracts be tested and audited?

   A. To make them look nice

   B. To ensure they function correctly, are free from vulnerabilities, and comply with best practices

   C. To make them easier to read

Answers

1. **B** - To protect the network from attacks and ensure its integrity by using strong consensus mechanisms, software updates, and monitoring
2. **B** - To ensure all participants agree on the state of the network and make decisions fairly and securely
3. **B** - To fix vulnerabilities and improve security, keeping the network's defenses strong
4. **B** - It watches for unusual behavior, alerting to potential threats so they can be addressed quickly

5. **B** - To ensure they function correctly, are free from vulnerabilities, and comply with best practices

Cloaked in Coins

A loud splash erupted from the riverbank as a feathered hat-wearing rabbit tumbled into the water, clutching a scroll. Robbie Rabbit, ever the eager explorer, bounded out of the water and waved the scroll in front of Barry Bear.

"Barry! You've got to see this! The Wise Old Wizard has sent us on another quest!" Robbie exclaimed, shaking water droplets everywhere.

Barry, engrossed in arranging his honey jars, looked up with a smile. "What is it about this time, Robbie?"

"It's about privacy coins! We need to learn about Monero, Zcash, and Dash!" Robbie said, eyes twinkling with excitement.

"Privacy coins? That sounds intriguing," Barry replied, setting aside his honey jar.

They made their way to the Wise Old Wizard's tower, where the Wizard greeted them warmly, his eyes sparkling with wisdom.

"Ah, Barry and Robbie, welcome," the Wizard began. "Today, we will explore the world of privacy coins, focusing on Monero, Zcash, and Dash."

Barry tilted his head. "What are privacy coins, and how do they work?"

The Wizard nodded. "Privacy coins are special kinds of tokens designed to keep transactions private and untraceable. They use advanced techniques to hide transaction details from prying eyes (privacy coins)."

Robbie's ears perked up. "So, they help keep our transactions secret?"

"Exactly, Robbie," the Wizard replied. "Let's start with Monero. Monero uses a technique called ring signatures to mix a user's transaction with a group of others, making it very difficult to trace (ring signatures)."

With a wave of the Wizard's staff, a shimmering portal opened, leading them into a bustling market where various creatures traded goods.

"First, let's explore Monero," the Wizard said, leading them to a stall where a fox was making a transaction. "Monero ensures privacy by mixing transactions together, making it hard to tell who is sending what to whom."

Barry watched as the fox's transaction was obscured by a flurry of other transactions. "So, it's like hiding your message in a crowd?"

"Precisely, Barry," the Wizard replied. "Next, let's look at Zcash. Zcash offers the option to use shielded transactions, which hide the sender, recipient, and amount of the transaction using advanced cryptographic techniques (shielded transactions)."

They moved to another stall where a rabbit was using Zcash to buy some enchanted herbs. "Zcash allows users to choose between transparent and shielded transactions, giving them flexibility in their privacy (flexible privacy)."

Robbie sniffed the air. "How does it keep everything hidden?"

The Wizard smiled. "Zcash uses a method called zk-SNARKs, which stands for zero-knowledge succinct non-interactive arguments of knowledge. This allows transactions to be verified without revealing any details (zk-SNARKs)."

Barry saw the rabbit's transaction disappear into a magical shield. "So, it's like a magic cloak that hides everything?"

"Exactly," the Wizard replied. "Now, let's talk about Dash. Dash offers a feature called PrivateSend, which mixes transactions together to enhance privacy (PrivateSend)."

They arrived at a stall where a pixie was using Dash to buy a magical potion. "PrivateSend mixes transactions from multiple users, making it hard to trace the origin of each transaction (transaction mixing)."

Robbie clapped his paws. "This is amazing! Are there any other benefits?"

The Wizard nodded. "Dash also focuses on fast and low-cost transactions, making it practical for everyday use (fast transactions)."

Barry and Robbie spent the rest of the day exploring the world of privacy coins, amazed by the different techniques used to ensure privacy and security. By the time the sun began to set, they felt enlightened and excited about the possibilities.

As they made their way back through the portal, Robbie couldn't help but make Barry laugh with his impressions of the Wise Old Wizard explaining privacy coins.

Barry, feeling wiser and more secure, knew that with the knowledge of these privacy coins, they could explore and transact in ways they had never imagined.

Explanation of Concepts

1. **Privacy Coins**: Special kinds of tokens designed to keep transactions private and untraceable. They use advanced techniques to hide transaction details from prying eyes, ensuring that users' financial activities remain confidential.
2. **Monero**: A privacy coin that uses ring signatures to mix a user's transaction with a group of others. This makes it very difficult to trace who is sending what to whom, enhancing the privacy of transactions.
3. **Ring Signatures**: A cryptographic technique used by Monero to mix transactions together. It hides the sender's identity by making their transaction indistinguishable from a group of others, providing strong privacy.
4. **Zcash**: A privacy coin that offers the option to use shielded transactions, which hide the sender, recipient, and amount of the transaction. It uses advanced cryptographic techniques to ensure privacy and security.
5. **Shielded Transactions**: Transactions in Zcash that hide all details, including the sender, recipient, and amount. Users can choose between transparent and shielded transactions, depending on their privacy needs.
6. **zk-SNARKs**: Zero-knowledge succinct non-interactive arguments of knowledge, a method used by Zcash to verify transactions without revealing any details. It allows for private transactions while ensuring their validity.

7. **Dash**: A privacy coin that offers a feature called PrivateSend, which mixes transactions from multiple users. This makes it difficult to trace the origin of each transaction, enhancing privacy.
8. **PrivateSend**: A feature in Dash that mixes transactions to obscure their origins. It enhances privacy by making it difficult to trace individual transactions back to their source.
9. **Fast Transactions**: Dash focuses on fast and low-cost transactions, making it practical for everyday use. This ensures that users can quickly and efficiently conduct transactions while maintaining privacy.

Questions

1. What are privacy coins designed to do?

    A. Make transactions faster

    B. Keep transactions private and untraceable

    C. Increase the number of tokens

2. How does Monero ensure the privacy of its users' transactions?

    A. By using ring signatures to mix a user's transaction with a group of others

    B. By making transactions public

    C. By increasing the transaction fees

3. What is the unique feature of Zcash that allows for private transactions?

    A. Transparent transactions

    B. Ring signatures

    C. Shielded transactions using zk-SNARKs

4. What is the purpose of Dash's PrivateSend feature?

    A. To mix transactions from multiple users and make them harder to trace

    B. To speed up the transaction process

C. To increase the value of the tokens

5. Which privacy coin gives users the option to choose between transparent and shielded transactions?

   A. Monero

   B. Zcash

   C. Dash

Answers

1. **B** - Keep transactions private and untraceable
2. **A** - By using ring signatures to mix a user's transaction with a group of others
3. **C** - Shielded transactions using zk-SNARKs
4. **A** - To mix transactions from multiple users and make them harder to trace
5. **B** - Zcash

Hushed Transactions

A bright flash of light illuminated the forest as a feathered hat-wearing rabbit emerged from a hollow log, clutching an ancient scroll. Robbie Rabbit, with his boundless enthusiasm, darted over to Barry Bear, waving the scroll excitedly.

"Barry! You've got to see this! The Wise Old Wizard has sent us on another quest!" Robbie exclaimed, bouncing up and down.

Barry, engrossed in arranging his honey jars, looked up with a smile. "What's it about this time, Robbie?"

"It's about privacy technologies! We need to learn about zk-SNARKs, ring signatures, and stealth addresses!" Robbie said, his eyes twinkling with curiosity.

"Privacy technologies? That sounds intriguing," Barry replied, already interested.

They made their way to the Wise Old Wizard's tower, where the Wizard greeted them warmly, his eyes twinkling with knowledge.

"Ah, Barry and Robbie, welcome," the Wizard began. "Today, we will explore the world of privacy technologies, focusing on zk-SNARKs, ring signatures, and stealth addresses."

Barry tilted his head. "What are these privacy technologies, and how do they work?"

The Wizard nodded. "These technologies are designed to keep transactions and data private and secure. Let's start with zk-SNARKs. This stands for zero-knowledge succinct non-interactive arguments of knowledge, a method that allows transactions to be verified without revealing any details (zk-SNARKs)."

Robbie's ears perked up. "So, it's like a secret code that only the right person can understand?"

"Exactly, Robbie," the Wizard replied. "Let's explore how zk-SNARKs work."

With a wave of the Wizard's staff, a shimmering portal opened, leading them into a grand library filled with ancient scrolls and magical tomes.

"First, let's explore zk-SNARKs," the Wizard said, leading them to a table where a fox was studying a scroll. "zk-SNARKs allow a user to prove that they know a value without revealing the value itself. It's like showing you have the correct answer to a puzzle without showing the puzzle or the answer."

Barry watched as the fox used zk-SNARKs to verify a transaction without revealing any details. "So, it keeps everything secret while still proving it's correct?"

"Precisely, Barry," the Wizard replied. "Next, let's look at ring signatures. Ring signatures are used to mix a user's transaction with a group of others, making it very difficult to trace who is sending what to whom (ring signatures)."

They moved to another section of the library where a rabbit was demonstrating ring signatures. "Ring signatures create a digital signature from a group of possible signers, but it is not clear which member of the group actually produced the signature," the Wizard explained.

Robbie hopped around the demonstration. "So, it's like hiding your message in a crowd?"

"Exactly," the Wizard replied. "This ensures that the sender remains anonymous while still validating the transaction."

They moved on to a grand hall where creatures traded various goods. "Now, let's explore stealth addresses. Stealth addresses are used to receive payments without revealing the recipient's public address (stealth addresses)."

Barry saw a pixie using a stealth address to receive a payment. "How does that work?"

The Wizard nodded. "Stealth addresses allow a sender to create a unique, one-time address for each transaction on behalf of the recipient. This ensures that the recipient's public address remains hidden, enhancing privacy."

Robbie clapped his paws. "This is amazing! Are there any other benefits?"

The Wizard smiled. "Yes, stealth addresses also prevent others from linking multiple transactions to the same recipient, ensuring complete privacy for the recipient's activities."

Barry and Robbie spent the rest of the day exploring the world of privacy technologies, amazed by the different techniques used to ensure privacy and security. By the time the sun began to set, they felt enlightened and excited about the possibilities.

As they made their way back through the portal, Robbie couldn't help but make Barry laugh with his impressions of the Wise Old Wizard explaining privacy technologies.

Barry, feeling wiser and more secure, knew that with the knowledge of these privacy technologies, they could explore and transact in ways they had never imagined.

Explanation of Concepts

1. **zk-SNARKs**: Zero-knowledge succinct non-interactive arguments of knowledge, a cryptographic method that allows one party to prove to another that they know a value without revealing any information about the value itself. This technique ensures privacy while verifying transactions.
2. **Ring Signatures**: A cryptographic technique that mixes a user's transaction with a group of others, making it very difficult to trace who is sending what to whom. It provides anonymity for the sender while still validating the transaction.
3. **Stealth Addresses**: A method used to receive payments without revealing the recipient's public address. It allows a sender to create a unique, one-time address for each transaction, ensuring that the recipient's public address remains hidden and enhancing privacy.
4. **Privacy Technologies**: These are advanced cryptographic techniques designed to keep transactions and data private and secure. They ensure that users' financial activities remain confidential and untraceable.
5. **Transaction Verification**: The process of proving that a transaction is valid without revealing any details. zk-SNARKs are an example of a technology that allows transaction verification while maintaining privacy.
6. **Anonymity**: The state of being anonymous, which means that one's identity is not known. Ring signatures provide anonymity for the sender by making it difficult to trace the origin of a transaction.

7. **Enhanced Privacy**: Technologies like stealth addresses ensure that multiple transactions cannot be linked to the same recipient, providing complete privacy for the recipient's activities and ensuring confidentiality.

Questions

1. What do privacy technologies like zk-SNARKs, ring signatures, and stealth addresses help to do?

    A. Make transactions faster

    B. Keep transactions and data private and secure

    C. Increase the number of tokens in a network

2. What does zk-SNARKs allow a user to do?

    A. Reveal all transaction details to everyone

    B. Prove that they know a value without revealing any information about the value itself

    C. Create multiple transactions at once

3. How do ring signatures provide anonymity for the sender?

    A. By mixing the sender's transaction with a group of others, making it difficult to trace who sent what

    B. By hiding the transaction completely

    C. By encrypting the sender's name only

4. What is the main function of stealth addresses?

    A. To make transactions faster

B. To receive payments without revealing the recipient's public address

C. To duplicate transactions

5. Why are stealth addresses useful for enhancing privacy?

    A. They prevent multiple transactions from being linked to the same recipient

    B. They make the transaction process more complicated

    C. They allow the sender to remain anonymous

Answers

1. **B** - Keep transactions and data private and secure
2. **B** - Prove that they know a value without revealing any information about the value itself
3. **A** - By mixing the sender's transaction with a group of others, making it difficult to trace who sent what
4. **B** - To receive payments without revealing the recipient's public address
5. **A** - They prevent multiple transactions from being linked to the same recipient

Stable Shifts Ahead

A sudden gust of wind sent a swirl of leaves dancing across the forest floor. Robbie Rabbit, with his ever-present feathered hat, darted out from behind a tree, clutching a scroll tightly in his paw.

"Barry! The Wise Old Wizard has sent us another quest!" Robbie exclaimed, hopping excitedly.

Barry, arranging his collection of shiny pebbles, looked up with a smile. "What's it about this time, Robbie?"

"It's about stablecoins! We need to learn about fiat-collateralized, crypto-collateralized, and algorithmic stablecoins!" Robbie said, his eyes twinkling with curiosity.

"Stablecoins? That sounds intriguing," Barry replied, already interested.

They made their way to the Wise Old Wizard's tower, where the Wizard greeted them warmly, his eyes sparkling with knowledge.

"Ah, Barry and Robbie, welcome," the Wizard began. "Today, we will explore the world of stablecoins, focusing on fiat-collateralized, crypto-collateralized, and algorithmic stablecoins."

Barry tilted his head. "What are stablecoins, and how do they work?"

The Wizard nodded. "Stablecoins are special kinds of tokens designed to maintain a stable value. They are pegged to other assets to reduce volatility. Let's start with fiat-collateralized stablecoins. These are backed by traditional currencies like the dollar, held in reserve (backed by traditional currency)."

Robbie's ears perked up. "So, they have real money backing them?"

"Exactly, Robbie," the Wizard replied. "Let's explore how fiat-collateralized stablecoins work."

With a wave of the Wizard's staff, a shimmering portal opened, leading them into a bustling market filled with traders.

"First, let's explore fiat-collateralized stablecoins," the Wizard said, leading them to a stall where a fox was exchanging tokens for dollars. "These stablecoins are backed by an equivalent amount of fiat currency held in reserve. For every token issued, there is a dollar kept safe somewhere."

Barry watched as the fox exchanged tokens for dollars. "So, if you have one of these tokens, it's always worth one dollar?"

"Precisely, Barry," the Wizard replied. "Next, let's look at crypto-collateralized stablecoins. These are backed by other cryptocurrencies instead of traditional currency (backed by other cryptocurrencies)."

They moved to another stall where a rabbit was using a basket of different coins to back his tokens. "Crypto-collateralized stablecoins require users to deposit cryptocurrencies as collateral, often more than the value of the stablecoins issued to account for volatility," the Wizard explained.

Robbie hopped around the stall. "So, you need to put in more crypto to get these tokens?"

"Exactly," the Wizard replied. "This over-collateralization helps protect the value of the stablecoins even if the price of the collateral drops."

They moved on to a grand hall where creatures were trading various assets. "Now, let's explore algorithmic stablecoins. These are not backed by any collateral but instead use algorithms to control their supply (algorithm-controlled supply)."

Barry saw a pixie adjusting the number of tokens in circulation based on market demand. "How does that work?"

The Wizard nodded. "Algorithmic stablecoins use smart contracts to automatically increase or decrease the supply of tokens based on demand. If the price goes above the target, more tokens are created. If it falls below, tokens are bought back and removed from circulation (smart contract adjustments)."

Robbie clapped his paws. "This is amazing! Are there any risks?"

The Wizard smiled. "Each type of stablecoin has its own risks. Fiat-collateralized stablecoins rely on the trustworthiness of the entity holding the reserves. Crypto-collateralized stablecoins are exposed to cryptocurrency volatility, and algorithmic stablecoins depend on the effectiveness of their algorithms (different types of risks)."

Barry and Robbie spent the rest of the day exploring the world of stablecoins, amazed by the different mechanisms used to maintain their value. By the time the sun began to set, they felt enlightened and excited about the possibilities.

As they made their way back through the portal, Robbie couldn't help but make Barry laugh with his impressions of the Wise Old Wizard explaining stablecoins.

Barry, feeling wiser and more informed, knew that with the knowledge of these stablecoins, they could explore and transact in ways they had never imagined.

Explanation of Concepts

1. **Stablecoins**: Special kinds of tokens designed to maintain a stable value. They are pegged to other assets to reduce volatility, making them a reliable medium of exchange or store of value.
2. **Fiat-Collateralized Stablecoins**: Stablecoins backed by traditional currencies like the dollar, held in reserve. For every token issued, there is an equivalent amount of fiat currency kept safe, ensuring the token's value remains stable.
3. **Crypto-Collateralized Stablecoins**: Stablecoins backed by other cryptocurrencies instead of traditional currency. Users deposit cryptocurrencies as collateral, often more than the value of the stablecoins issued, to account for the volatility of the collateral.
4. **Algorithmic Stablecoins**: Stablecoins that are not backed by any collateral but use algorithms to control their supply. Smart contracts automatically increase or decrease the supply of tokens based on market demand to maintain a stable value.
5. **Backed by Traditional Currency**: Fiat-collateralized stablecoins have real money backing them, meaning they are always worth the amount of currency held in reserve.
6. **Backed by Other Cryptocurrencies**: Crypto-collateralized stablecoins use a basket of different cryptocurrencies as collateral. The value of these stablecoins is protected by over-collateralization, ensuring stability even with cryptocurrency volatility.

7. **Algorithm-Controlled Supply**: Algorithmic stablecoins use smart contracts to adjust the supply of tokens automatically. If demand increases, more tokens are created. If demand decreases, tokens are bought back and removed from circulation to maintain stability.
8. **Smart Contract Adjustments**: The process by which algorithmic stablecoins adjust their supply. Smart contracts respond to market conditions, creating or destroying tokens as needed to keep the price stable.
9. **Different Types of Risks**: Each type of stablecoin has its own risks. Fiat-collateralized stablecoins depend on the trustworthiness of the entity holding the reserves, crypto-collateralized stablecoins face cryptocurrency volatility, and algorithmic stablecoins rely on the effectiveness of their algorithms.

Questions

1. What are stablecoins designed to do?

    A. Make transactions faster

    B. Maintain a stable value by being pegged to other assets

    C. Increase in value over time

2. What backs fiat-collateralized stablecoins?

    A. Traditional currencies like the dollar, held in reserve

    B. A basket of other cryptocurrencies

    C. Magic spells

3. Why do crypto-collateralized stablecoins often require over-collateralization?

    A. To make the tokens look more valuable

    B. To protect the value of the stablecoins in case the price of the collateral drops

    C. To create more tokens

4. How do algorithmic stablecoins maintain their value?

    A. By being backed by gold

B. By adjusting the supply of tokens automatically using smart contracts based on market demand

C. By locking tokens away in a vault

5. What is one risk associated with fiat-collateralized stablecoins?

    A. The algorithms might fail

    B. The price of cryptocurrencies might drop

    C. They rely on the trustworthiness of the entity holding the reserves

Answers

1. **B** - Maintain a stable value by being pegged to other assets
2. **A** - Traditional currencies like the dollar, held in reserve
3. **B** - To protect the value of the stablecoins in case the price of the collateral drops
4. **B** - By adjusting the supply of tokens automatically using smart contracts based on market demand
5. **C** - They rely on the trustworthiness of the entity holding the reserves

Taming the Tokens

The forest hummed with the cheerful chatter of chirping birds and the gentle rustle of leaves. Out of nowhere, a dazzling flash of light swept across the clearing, revealing a rabbit with a feathered hat stepping out from behind a tree. He clutched a scroll tightly in his paw, his eyes wide with excitement.

"Barry! You've got to see this! The Wise Old Wizard has sent us another quest!" Robbie Rabbit exclaimed, hopping excitedly.

Barry Bear, who was arranging his collection of shiny pebbles, looked up with a smile. "What's it about this time, Robbie?"

"It's about stablecoins! We need to learn about their practical applications and challenges!" Robbie said, his eyes twinkling with curiosity.

"Stablecoins? That sounds intriguing," Barry replied, already interested.

They made their way to the Wise Old Wizard's tower, where the Wizard greeted them warmly, his eyes sparkling with knowledge.

"Ah, Barry and Robbie, welcome," the Wizard began. "Today, we will explore the practical applications of stablecoins and the challenges they face."

Barry tilted his head. "What are stablecoins, and how are they used?"

The Wizard nodded. "Stablecoins are special kinds of tokens designed to maintain a stable value. They are used in various ways, from facilitating payments to providing a stable store of value (stable value)."

Robbie's ears perked up. "So, they have lots of uses?"

"Exactly, Robbie," the Wizard replied. "Let's start with payments. Stablecoins can be used to make quick and low-cost transactions, both locally and internationally (payments)."

With a wave of the Wizard's staff, a shimmering portal opened, leading them into a bustling market filled with traders.

"First, let's explore how stablecoins are used for payments," the Wizard said, leading them to a stall where a fox was buying goods using stablecoins. "Stablecoins allow for fast and low-cost transactions, making them ideal for everyday purchases and international remittances."

Barry watched as the fox completed a transaction in seconds. "So, they're like using regular money but faster and cheaper?"

"Precisely, Barry," the Wizard replied. "Next, let's look at their use in decentralized finance, or DeFi. Stablecoins are often used as collateral for loans, providing a stable value that protects both lenders and borrowers (collateral)."

They moved to another stall where a rabbit was using stablecoins to secure a loan. "In DeFi, stablecoins can be used to earn interest, borrow against, or even trade without the risk of high volatility," the Wizard explained.

Robbie hopped around the stall. "So, they make borrowing and lending safer?"

"Exactly," the Wizard replied. "Stablecoins also provide a stable store of value, making them a good option for saving and protecting against inflation (store of value)."

They arrived at a grand hall where creatures were saving their earnings in stablecoins. "By using stablecoins, individuals can protect their savings from the effects of inflation and currency devaluation," the Wizard explained.

Barry saw a pixie saving her earnings in stablecoins. "So, they keep your money safe from losing value?"

"Precisely," the Wizard replied. "Now, let's talk about the challenges. One major challenge is regulatory scrutiny. Because stablecoins can be used globally, they must comply with various regulations (regulatory compliance)."

Robbie clapped his paws. "That sounds tricky! How do they manage that?"

The Wizard nodded. "It requires constant monitoring and adaptation to different regulatory environments. Another challenge is maintaining trust in the reserves that back stablecoins. Users need to be confident that the stablecoins are fully backed by the promised assets (trust in reserves)."

Barry and Robbie spent the rest of the day exploring the world of stablecoins, amazed by their practical applications and the challenges they face. By the time the sun began to set, they felt enlightened and excited about the possibilities.

As they made their way back through the portal, Robbie couldn't help but make Barry laugh with his impressions of the Wise Old Wizard explaining stablecoins.

Barry, feeling wiser and more informed, knew that with the knowledge of these stablecoins, they could explore and transact in ways they had never imagined.

Explanation of Concepts

1. **Stable Value:** Stablecoins are designed to maintain a stable value, reducing the volatility commonly associated with other tokens. They achieve this by being pegged to a stable asset, such as a traditional currency or a basket of assets.
2. **Payments:** Stablecoins are used for quick and low-cost transactions, making them ideal for everyday purchases and international remittances. They allow for fast and inexpensive transfers of value, both locally and globally.
3. **Collateral:** In decentralized finance (DeFi), stablecoins are often used as collateral for loans. They provide a stable value that protects both lenders and borrowers from the risk of high volatility, ensuring safer financial transactions.
4. **Store of Value:** Stablecoins provide a stable store of value, making them a good option for saving and protecting against inflation. They help individuals preserve their wealth by protecting their savings from the effects of inflation and currency devaluation.
5. **Regulatory Compliance:** One of the challenges stablecoins face is regulatory scrutiny. Because they can be used globally, they must comply with various regulations. This requires constant monitoring and adaptation to different regulatory environments.
6. **Trust in Reserves:** Maintaining trust in the reserves that back stablecoins is crucial. Users need to be confident that the stablecoins are fully backed by the promised assets, ensuring their value remains stable and

reliable. This trust is essential for the widespread adoption and use of stablecoins.

7. **DeFi (Decentralized Finance)**: A financial system built on blockchain technology that allows for peer-to-peer transactions without intermediaries. Stablecoins play a significant role in DeFi by providing a stable medium of exchange and collateral for various financial services.

Questions

1. What is the primary purpose of stablecoins?

    A. To increase in value over time

    B. To maintain a stable value by being pegged to a stable asset

    C. To make transactions slower

2. How are stablecoins used in payments?

    A. They allow for fast and low-cost transactions, both locally and internationally

    B. They are used to store goods in a market

    C. They are used to buy only digital items

3. What role do stablecoins play in decentralized finance (DeFi)?

    A. They are used as a form of entertainment

    B. They serve as collateral for loans, providing a stable value that protects lenders and borrowers

    C. They are used to create volatility in the market

4. Why are stablecoins considered a good store of value?

A. They help individuals protect their savings from inflation and currency devaluation

B. They lose value over time

C. They are always increasing in price

5. What is one of the main challenges faced by stablecoins?

A. They need to be faster than other tokens

B. They must comply with various regulations globally, requiring constant monitoring and adaptation

C. They are too easy to use

Answers

1. **B** - To maintain a stable value by being pegged to a stable asset
2. **A** - They allow for fast and low-cost transactions, both locally and internationally
3. **B** - They serve as collateral for loans, providing a stable value that protects lenders and borrowers
4. **A** - They help individuals protect their savings from inflation and currency devaluation
5. **B** - They must comply with various regulations globally, requiring constant monitoring and adaptation

Hat Tricks & Tokens

A brilliant sunbeam sliced through the dense forest canopy, casting its golden light upon a clearing where Robbie Rabbit, utterly absorbed in a scroll, sat with fervent concentration. The feathered hat perched precariously atop his head tipped at a jaunty angle as he enthusiastically waved the scroll at Barry Bear, who, nearby, busily collected a handful of glittering pebbles.

"Barry! You've got to see this! The Wise Old Wizard has sent us on another quest!" Robbie exclaimed, practically vibrating with excitement.

Barry, ever patient, looked up with a smile. "What's it about this time, Robbie?"

"It's about something called Non-Fungible Tokens, or NFTs! We need to learn what they are and how they work!" Robbie said, his eyes twinkling with curiosity.

"NFTs? That sounds intriguing," Barry replied, setting aside his pebbles.

They made their way to the Wise Old Wizard's tower, where the Wizard greeted them warmly, his eyes sparkling with knowledge.

"Ah, Barry and Robbie, welcome," the Wizard began. "Today, we will explore the world of Non-Fungible Tokens, or NFTs, and understand their significance."

Barry tilted his head. "What are NFTs, and how do they work?"

The Wizard nodded. "NFTs are unique digital items that represent ownership or proof of authenticity for a particular item. Unlike regular tokens, which are identical and interchangeable, each NFT is one-of-a-kind (unique digital items)."

Robbie's ears perked up. "So, they're like digital collectibles?"

"Exactly, Robbie," the Wizard replied. "Let's start with the basics. NFTs are built on specific standards that define how they operate and ensure they are unique. One of the most common standards is called ERC-721 (standard)."

With a wave of the Wizard's staff, a shimmering portal opened, leading them into a grand gallery filled with digital art and collectibles.

"First, let's explore the ERC-721 standard," the Wizard said, leading them to a pedestal displaying a glowing, digital painting. "ERC-721 is a set of guidelines that ensures each token created is unique and can be owned by only one person at a time (ownership)."

Barry watched as a fox admired the digital painting, which was displayed alongside a certificate of ownership. "So, this standard makes sure each item is one-of-a-kind and can be bought or sold?"

"Precisely, Barry," the Wizard replied. "Another important standard is ERC-1155. This one allows for the creation of both unique items and identical ones, making it more flexible for different types of digital assets (flexibility)."

They moved to another section of the gallery where a rabbit was showcasing a collection of virtual trading cards. "ERC-1155 lets creators produce both unique and identical items, depending on what they need," the Wizard explained.

Robbie hopped around the gallery. "So, what can NFTs be used for?"

The Wizard smiled. "NFTs have many practical applications. They can be used to represent digital art, collectibles, virtual real estate, and even in-game items (applications)."

They arrived at a hall where creatures were trading various digital items. "NFTs allow artists to sell their work directly to collectors, providing proof of authenticity and ownership," the Wizard explained.

Barry saw a pixie trading a virtual sword that was used in a popular game. "So, they can be anything from art to game items?"

"Exactly," the Wizard replied. "Now, let's talk about the challenges. One major challenge is the environmental impact. Creating and trading NFTs requires a lot of energy, which can harm the environment (environmental impact)."

Robbie clapped his paws. "That sounds serious! How can we solve that?"

The Wizard nodded. "It requires ongoing research and development to find more energy-efficient methods. Another challenge is ensuring the security of NFTs. Because they are valuable, they can be targets for theft or fraud (security)."

Barry and Robbie spent the rest of the day exploring the world of NFTs, amazed by their versatility and the challenges they face. By the time the sun began to set, they felt enlightened and excited about the possibilities.

As they made their way back through the portal, Robbie couldn't help but make Barry laugh with his impressions of the Wise Old Wizard explaining NFTs.

Barry, feeling wiser and more informed, knew that with the knowledge of these tokens, they could explore and create in ways they had never imagined.

Explanation of Concepts

1. **Unique Digital Items**: NFTs are digital assets that represent ownership or proof of authenticity for a particular item. Unlike regular tokens, which are identical and interchangeable, each NFT is one-of-a-kind.
2. **Standard**: NFTs are built on specific standards that define how they operate and ensure they are unique. ERC-721 is one of the most common standards, ensuring each token created is unique and can be owned by only one person at a time.
3. **Ownership**: The ERC-721 standard ensures that each NFT is unique and can be owned by only one person at a time. This makes NFTs valuable as digital collectibles or proof of ownership for digital items.
4. **Flexibility**: ERC-1155 is another important standard that allows for the creation of both unique items and identical ones. This flexibility makes it suitable for different types of digital assets, such as virtual trading cards or in-game items.
5. **Applications**: NFTs have many practical applications, including representing digital art, collectibles, virtual real estate, and in-game items. They provide a way for creators to sell their work directly to collectors and offer proof of authenticity and ownership.
6. **Environmental Impact**: One major challenge of NFTs is their environmental impact. Creating and trading NFTs requires a lot of energy, which can harm the

environment. Finding more energy-efficient methods is an ongoing research and development effort.
7. **Security**: Ensuring the security of NFTs is crucial because they are valuable. They can be targets for theft or fraud, so protecting them with secure technologies and practices is essential to maintaining their value and trustworthiness.

Questions

1. What makes NFTs different from regular tokens?

    A. NFTs are identical and interchangeable

    B. NFTs are unique digital items that represent ownership or proof of authenticity

    C. NFTs can only be used in games

2. What is the ERC-721 standard used for?

    A. It allows for creating identical digital items

    B. It ensures each NFT is unique and can be owned by only one person at a time

    C. It makes NFTs less valuable

3. What can NFTs be used to represent?

    A. Only digital art

    B. Physical objects like furniture

    C. Digital art, collectibles, virtual real estate, and in-game items

4. What is one challenge associated with NFTs mentioned in the story?

    A. They are too difficult to create

B. They have a significant environmental impact due to the energy required for their creation and trading

C. They cannot be traded between users

5. Why is security important for NFTs?

    A. Because they are easy to make

    B. Because they are valuable and can be targets for theft or fraud

    C. Because they don't have any real-world value

Answers

1. **B** - NFTs are unique digital items that represent ownership or proof of authenticity
2. **B** - It ensures each NFT is unique and can be owned by only one person at a time
3. **C** - Digital art, collectibles, virtual real estate, and in-game items
4. **B** - They have a significant environmental impact due to the energy required for their creation and trading
5. **B** - Because they are valuable and can be targets for theft or fraud

Magic in the Digital Gallery

A dazzling ray of sunlight broke through the dense canopy, casting a golden glow on a peculiar scene. Robbie Rabbit, wearing his ever-present feathered hat, emerged from behind a tree, holding a scroll aloft.

"Barry! The Wise Old Wizard has sent us on another quest!" Robbie exclaimed, bouncing with excitement.

Barry Bear, busy arranging his collection of shiny pebbles, looked up with a smile. "What's it about this time, Robbie?"

"It's about something called Non-Fungible Tokens, or NFTs! We need to learn about their uses in art, gaming, and real estate!" Robbie said, his eyes twinkling with curiosity.

"NFTs? That sounds intriguing," Barry replied, setting aside his pebbles.

They made their way to the Wise Old Wizard's tower, where the Wizard greeted them warmly, his eyes sparkling with knowledge.

"Ah, Barry and Robbie, welcome," the Wizard began. "Today, we will explore the fascinating world of Non-Fungible Tokens, or NFTs, and their various uses."

Barry tilted his head. "What are NFTs, and how are they used?"

The Wizard nodded. "NFTs are unique digital items that represent ownership or proof of authenticity for a particular item. Unlike regular tokens, which are identical and interchangeable, each NFT is one-of-a-kind (unique digital items)."

Robbie's ears perked up. "So, they're like digital collectibles?"

"Exactly, Robbie," the Wizard replied. "Let's start with how NFTs are used in the world of art. NFTs allow artists to sell their digital creations directly to collectors, providing proof of ownership and authenticity (digital art)."

With a wave of the Wizard's staff, a shimmering portal opened, leading them into a grand gallery filled with digital paintings and sculptures.

"First, let's explore digital art," the Wizard said, leading them to a pedestal displaying a glowing, digital painting. "NFTs ensure that each piece of digital art is unique and owned by only one person at a time. This makes it valuable as a collectible."

Barry watched as a fox admired the digital painting, which was displayed alongside a certificate of ownership. "So, this standard makes sure each item is one-of-a-kind and can be bought or sold?"

"Precisely, Barry," the Wizard replied. "Next, let's look at NFTs in gaming. NFTs can represent in-game items like weapons, armor, or virtual land, giving players true ownership and the ability to trade these items (in-game items)."

They moved to another section of the gallery where a rabbit was showcasing a collection of virtual swords and shields. "In gaming, NFTs allow players to own and trade unique items that enhance their gaming experience," the Wizard explained.

Robbie hopped around the gallery. "So, what else can NFTs be used for?"

The Wizard smiled. "NFTs are also used in virtual real estate. People can buy, sell, and trade virtual land or property, just like in the real world (virtual real estate)."

They arrived at a grand hall where creatures were trading virtual land deeds. "NFTs allow for the ownership of virtual spaces in online worlds, creating new opportunities for investment and development," the Wizard explained.

Barry saw a pixie trading a deed for a virtual castle. "So, they can be anything from art to game items to virtual land?"

"Exactly," the Wizard replied. "Now, let's talk about the challenges. One major challenge is ensuring the security of NFTs. Because they are valuable, they can be targets for theft or fraud (security)."

Robbie clapped his paws. "That sounds serious! How can we solve that?"

The Wizard nodded. "It requires ongoing research and development to find more secure methods. Another challenge is the environmental impact. Creating and trading

NFTs requires a lot of energy, which can harm the environment (environmental impact)."

Barry and Robbie spent the rest of the day exploring the world of NFTs, amazed by their versatility and the challenges they face. By the time the sun began to set, they felt enlightened and excited about the possibilities.

As they made their way back through the portal, Robbie couldn't help but make Barry laugh with his impressions of the Wise Old Wizard explaining NFTs.

Barry, feeling wiser and more informed, knew that with the knowledge of these tokens, they could explore and create in ways they had never imagined.

Explanation of Concepts

1. **Unique Digital Items**: NFTs are digital assets that represent ownership or proof of authenticity for a particular item. Unlike regular tokens, which are identical and interchangeable, each NFT is one-of-a-kind.
2. **Digital Art**: NFTs allow artists to sell their digital creations directly to collectors, providing proof of ownership and authenticity. This makes each piece of digital art unique and valuable as a collectible.
3. **In-Game Items**: NFTs can represent in-game items like weapons, armor, or virtual land. They give players true ownership and the ability to trade these items, enhancing their gaming experience.
4. **Virtual Real Estate**: NFTs are used in virtual real estate, allowing people to buy, sell, and trade virtual land or property, just like in the real world. This creates new opportunities for investment and development in online worlds.
5. **Security**: Ensuring the security of NFTs is crucial because they are valuable. They can be targets for theft or fraud, so protecting them with secure technologies and practices is essential to maintaining their value and trustworthiness.
6. **Environmental Impact**: One major challenge of NFTs is their environmental impact. Creating and trading NFTs requires a lot of energy, which can harm the environment. Finding more energy-efficient methods is an ongoing research and development effort.

Questions

1. What is an NFT, and what makes it different from regular tokens?

    A. An NFT is a common digital token that is identical to others.

    B. An NFT is a unique digital item that represents ownership or proof of authenticity.

    C. An NFT is a physical coin that can be traded online.

2. How are NFTs used in the world of digital art?

    A. They are used to create identical copies of digital paintings.

    B. They allow artists to sell their digital creations directly to collectors, providing proof of ownership and authenticity.

    C. They are used to print physical versions of digital art.

3. What can NFTs represent in gaming?

    A. Common game currency that can be found by all players

    B. Unique in-game items like weapons, armor, or virtual land that players can own and trade

    C. The rules of the game

4. What is virtual real estate, and how do NFTs play a role in it?

    A. Virtual real estate refers to online spaces that people can buy, sell, and trade using NFTs, just like real-world property.

    B. Virtual real estate is where players build houses in video games without ownership.

    C. Virtual real estate is a concept unrelated to NFTs.

5. What are two challenges mentioned in the story that NFTs face?

    A. Lack of interest from collectors and no way to trade them

    B. Security concerns and environmental impact due to the high energy use required for creating and trading NFTs

    C. NFTs cannot be used for anything valuable and are difficult to understand

Answers

1. **B** - An NFT is a unique digital item that represents ownership or proof of authenticity.
2. **B** - They allow artists to sell their digital creations directly to collectors, providing proof of ownership and authenticity.
3. **B** - Unique in-game items like weapons, armor, or virtual land that players can own and trade.
4. **A** - Virtual real estate refers to online spaces that people can buy, sell, and trade using NFTs, just like real-world property.
5. **B** - Security concerns and environmental impact due to the high energy use required for creating and trading NFTs.

Tokens of Change

A sparkling brook chattered cheerfully as Robbie Rabbit, with his ever-present feathered hat perched jauntily atop his head, darted out from behind a tree. Clutching a scroll with great excitement, he hopped over to Barry Bear, who meticulously arranged his collection of gleaming pebbles.

"Barry! The Wise Old Wizard has sent us another quest!" Robbie exclaimed, practically bouncing with excitement.

Barry looked up with a smile. "What's it about this time, Robbie?"

"It's about Non-Fungible Tokens, or NFTs, and their economic and cultural impact!" Robbie said, his eyes twinkling with curiosity.

"NFTs? That sounds intriguing" Barry replied, setting aside his pebbles.

They made their way to the Wise Old Wizard's tower, where the Wizard greeted them warmly, his eyes sparkling with knowledge.

"Ah, Barry and Robbie, welcome," the Wizard began. "Today, we will explore the impact of Non-Fungible Tokens, or NFTs, on both our economy and culture."

Barry tilted his head. "What are NFTs, and how do they impact us?"

The Wizard nodded. "NFTs are unique digital items that represent ownership or proof of authenticity for a particular item. Their impact is both economic and cultural, affecting how we create, trade, and appreciate digital assets (unique digital items)."

Robbie's ears perked up. "So, they change the way we buy and sell things?"

"Exactly, Robbie," the Wizard replied. "Let's start with the economic implications. NFTs create new opportunities for artists and creators to monetize their work directly, bypassing traditional middlemen (monetization)."

With a wave of the Wizard's staff, a shimmering portal opened, leading them into a bustling marketplace filled with digital art and collectibles.

"First, let's explore the economic impact," the Wizard said, leading them to a stall where a fox was selling digital paintings. "Artists can now sell their work directly to collectors, keeping a larger share of the profits. This empowers creators and encourages more innovation."

Barry watched as the fox completed a sale and received payment instantly. "So, it helps artists make more money and reach more people?"

"Precisely, Barry," the Wizard replied. "NFTs also create new markets and investment opportunities. Collectors can buy, sell, and trade digital assets just like physical ones, potentially making a profit (new markets)."

They moved to another stall where a rabbit was trading virtual real estate. "NFTs allow for the creation of entirely new economies within digital worlds, where virtual goods and properties hold real value," the Wizard explained.

Robbie hopped around the stall. "So, they create new ways for people to invest and trade?"

"Exactly," the Wizard replied. "Now, let's talk about the cultural implications. NFTs are changing how we perceive and value digital art and collectibles (cultural value)."

They arrived at a grand gallery where creatures were admiring digital sculptures and paintings. "NFTs give digital art the same status and respect as traditional art forms, allowing artists to gain recognition and appreciation for their work," the Wizard explained.

Barry saw a pixie admiring a digital sculpture. "So, they help digital artists get the recognition they deserve?"

"Precisely," the Wizard replied. "NFTs also foster a sense of community and shared experience. Collectors and fans can connect directly with creators, participating in exclusive events and owning a piece of their favorite works (community)."

Robbie clapped his paws. "That sounds amazing! Are there any challenges?"

The Wizard nodded. "One major challenge is the environmental impact. Creating and trading NFTs requires a lot of energy, which can harm the environment (environmental impact)."

Barry and Robbie spent the rest of the day exploring the world of NFTs, amazed by their impact on both the economy and culture. By the time the sun began to set, they felt enlightened and excited about the possibilities.

As they made their way back through the portal, Robbie couldn't help but make Barry laugh with his impressions of the Wise Old Wizard explaining NFTs.

Barry, feeling wiser and more informed, knew that with the knowledge of these tokens, they could explore and create in ways they had never imagined.

Explanation of Concepts

1. **Unique Digital Items**: NFTs are digital assets that represent ownership or proof of authenticity for a particular item. Unlike regular tokens, which are identical and interchangeable, each NFT is one-of-a-kind.
2. **Monetization**: NFTs create new opportunities for artists and creators to monetize their work directly, bypassing traditional middlemen. This empowers creators and encourages more innovation by allowing them to keep a larger share of the profits.
3. **New Markets**: NFTs create new markets and investment opportunities. Collectors can buy, sell, and trade digital assets just like physical ones, potentially making a profit. This allows for the creation of entirely new economies within digital worlds.
4. **Cultural Value**: NFTs are changing how we perceive and value digital art and collectibles. They give digital art the same status and respect as traditional art forms, allowing artists to gain recognition and appreciation for their work.
5. **Community**: NFTs foster a sense of community and shared experience. Collectors and fans can connect directly with creators, participating in exclusive events and owning a piece of their favorite works. This strengthens the bond between creators and their audience.
6. **Environmental Impact**: One major challenge of NFTs is their environmental impact. Creating and trading

NFTs requires a lot of energy, which can harm the environment. Finding more energy-efficient methods is an ongoing research and development effort.

Questions

1. What is an NFT, and how is it different from regular tokens?

    A. NFTs are identical digital tokens that can be exchanged for one another.

    B. NFTs are unique digital items that represent ownership or proof of authenticity.

    C. NFTs are physical items that can be bought online.

2. How do NFTs impact the economy, especially for artists and creators?

    A. They make it harder for artists to sell their work.

    B. They allow artists to monetize their work directly, bypassing traditional middlemen and keeping more profits.

    C. They decrease the value of digital art.

3. What new opportunities do NFTs create in digital markets?

    A. They only allow for the trading of physical goods.

    B. They create new markets where digital assets can be bought, sold, and traded, similar to physical assets.

C. They eliminate the need for digital transactions altogether.

4. How are NFTs changing the cultural perception of digital art?

   A. They are making digital art less valuable than traditional art.

   B. They give digital art the same status and respect as traditional art forms, helping artists gain recognition.

   C. They make digital art harder to appreciate.

5. What is one of the challenges associated with NFTs mentioned in the story?

   A. They are too easy to create and trade.

   B. Their creation and trading require a lot of energy, which can have a negative environmental impact.

   C. They are not accepted by any digital marketplaces.

Answers

1. **B** - NFTs are unique digital items that represent ownership or proof of authenticity.

2. **B** - They allow artists to monetize their work directly, bypassing traditional middlemen and keeping more profits.
3. **B** - They create new markets where digital assets can be bought, sold, and traded, similar to physical assets.
4. **B** - They give digital art the same status and respect as traditional art forms, helping artists gain recognition.
5. **B** - Their creation and trading require a lot of energy, which can have a negative environmental impact.

Autonomy Unfurled

A brilliant shaft of sunlight wove its way through the thick forest canopy, bathing the lively clearing below in a golden glow. Robbie Rabbit, with his usual fervor, pored over an ancient scroll with an air of intense focus. With a sudden, eager bounce, he scurried over to where Barry Bear meticulously sorted his collection of glistening pebbles.

"Barry! You've got to see this! The Wise Old Wizard has sent us another quest!" Robbie exclaimed, his voice bubbling with excitement.

Barry looked up with a smile. "What's it about this time, Robbie?"

"It's about something called Decentralized Autonomous Organizations, or DAOs! We need to learn about their structure, operation, and some well-known examples!" Robbie said, his eyes twinkling with curiosity.

"DAOs? That sounds fascinating," Barry replied, setting aside his pebbles.

They made their way to the Wise Old Wizard's tower, where the Wizard greeted them warmly, his eyes sparkling with knowledge.

"Ah, Barry and Robbie, welcome," the Wizard began. "Today, we will explore the concept of Decentralized

Autonomous Organizations, or DAOs, and their significance."

Barry tilted his head. "What are DAOs, and how do they work?"

The Wizard nodded. "DAOs are organizations that operate based on rules encoded as computer programs. They are decentralized, meaning they don't have a central leader, and autonomous, meaning they can run themselves to a large extent (autonomous organization)."

Robbie's ears perked up. "So, they're like magical organizations that run themselves?"

"Exactly, Robbie," the Wizard replied. "Let's start with the structure and operation of DAOs. In a DAO, decisions are made by members who hold tokens, and these decisions are executed automatically by smart contracts (decision-making)."

With a wave of the Wizard's staff, a shimmering portal opened, leading them into a grand hall filled with creatures voting on various proposals.

"First, let's explore how decisions are made in a DAO," the Wizard said, leading them to a podium where a fox was casting a vote. "Members vote on proposals using tokens, and smart contracts automatically execute the decisions based on the vote results."

Barry watched as the fox's vote was counted and the proposal was implemented instantly. "So, the organization runs based on the votes of its members?"

"Precisely, Barry," the Wizard replied. "DAOs also operate transparently, as all transactions and decisions are recorded on a public ledger (transparency)."

They moved to another section of the hall where a rabbit was reviewing past decisions and transactions. "This transparency ensures that all actions are open to scrutiny, fostering trust among members," the Wizard explained.

Robbie hopped around the hall. "What are some examples of DAOs?"

The Wizard smiled. "Let's talk about some well-known DAOs and their impact. One of the first DAOs was simply called The DAO. It was created to act as a venture capital fund, allowing members to vote on investment proposals (venture capital)."

They arrived at a gallery showcasing various DAOs. "The DAO was an ambitious project, but it faced significant challenges, including a major security breach. Despite its difficulties, it set the stage for future DAOs (early challenges)."

Barry saw a display about MakerDAO, another well-known DAO. "What's this one about?"

"MakerDAO is a decentralized organization that manages a stable token and allows users to take out loans. Members vote on changes to the system, ensuring its stability and efficiency (stable token)."

Robbie clapped his paws. "That sounds amazing! Any other examples?"

The Wizard nodded. "Another interesting example is MolochDAO, which focuses on funding projects to improve the infrastructure of its network. It operates with a simple and efficient structure to make decision-making easier (funding projects)."

Barry and Robbie spent the rest of the day exploring the world of DAOs, amazed by their structure, operation, and impact. By the time the sun began to set, they felt enlightened and excited about the possibilities.

As they made their way back through the portal, Robbie couldn't help but make Barry laugh with his impressions of the Wise Old Wizard explaining DAOs.

Barry, feeling wiser and more informed, knew that with the knowledge of these organizations, they could explore and innovate in ways they had never imagined.

Explanation of Concepts

1. **Autonomous Organization**: DAOs are organizations that operate based on rules encoded as computer programs. They are decentralized, meaning they don't have a central leader, and autonomous, meaning they can run themselves to a large extent.
2. **Decision-Making**: In a DAO, decisions are made by members who hold tokens, and these decisions are executed automatically by smart contracts. This ensures that the organization operates based on the collective will of its members.
3. **Transparency**: DAOs operate transparently, as all transactions and decisions are recorded on a public ledger. This transparency fosters trust among members by ensuring that all actions are open to scrutiny.
4. **Venture Capital**: One of the first DAOs, called The DAO, was created to act as a venture capital fund. Members could vote on investment proposals, demonstrating the potential of DAOs to manage collective investments.
5. **Early Challenges**: The DAO faced significant challenges, including a major security breach. Despite its difficulties, it set the stage for future DAOs by highlighting the importance of security and governance.
6. **Stable Token**: MakerDAO is a well-known DAO that manages a stable token and allows users to take out loans. Members vote on changes to the system, ensuring its stability and efficiency.

7. **Funding Projects**: MolochDAO is another example of a DAO that focuses on funding projects to improve the infrastructure of its network. It operates with a simple and efficient structure to make decision-making easier.

Questions

1. What is a Decentralized Autonomous Organization (DAO)?

    A. A traditional organization with a central leader

    B. An organization that operates based on rules encoded as computer programs and runs itself without a central leader

    C. A government-run institution

2. How are decisions made in a DAO?

    A. By a central authority making all the decisions

    B. Through members voting on proposals, and decisions are executed automatically by smart contracts

    C. By random chance

3. Why is transparency important in a DAO?

    A. It ensures that decisions are hidden from members

    B. It allows all transactions and decisions to be recorded on a public ledger, fostering trust among members

    C. It makes decision-making slower and more complicated

4. What was The DAO, and what was its purpose?

   A. A traditional company that sold products online

   B. One of the first DAOs created to act as a venture capital fund, allowing members to vote on investment proposals

   C. A DAO designed for gaming purposes only

5. What is MakerDAO, and what does it manage?

   A. A DAO that manages a stable token and allows users to take out loans

   B. A platform for buying and selling real estate

   C. A social media network

Answers

1. **B** - An organization that operates based on rules encoded as computer programs and runs itself without a central leader.
2. **B** - Through members voting on proposals, and decisions are executed automatically by smart contracts.

3. **B** - It allows all transactions and decisions to be recorded on a public ledger, fostering trust among members.
4. **B** - One of the first DAOs created to act as a venture capital fund, allowing members to vote on investment proposals.
5. **A** - A DAO that manages a stable token and allows users to take out loans.

Bearly Decentralized

A rustling in the bushes caught the attention of a fox as it scurried through the forest. Moments later, Robbie Rabbit burst out, feathered hat askew, clutching an ancient scroll with great excitement. He bounded over to Barry Bear, who was meticulously stacking his collection of shiny pebbles.

"Barry! The Wise Old Wizard has sent us on another quest!" Robbie exclaimed, his voice bubbling with enthusiasm.

Barry looked up with a smile. "What's it about this time, Robbie?"

"It's about something called Web 3! We need to learn about its key features like decentralization, interactivity, user control, and more!" Robbie said, his eyes twinkling with curiosity.

"Web 3? That sounds fascinating," Barry replied, setting aside his pebbles.

They made their way to the Wise Old Wizard's tower, where the Wizard greeted them warmly, his eyes sparkling with wisdom.

"Ah, Barry and Robbie, welcome," the Wizard began. "Today, we will explore the fascinating world of Web 3 and understand its key features and implications."

Barry tilted his head. "What is Web 3, and how does it work?"

The Wizard nodded. "Web 3 is the next generation of the internet, designed to be more decentralized, interactive, and controlled by users. It's built on several key principles and technologies that empower individuals and enhance online experiences (next generation internet)."

Robbie's ears perked up. "So, it's like a magical new version of the internet?"

"Exactly, Robbie," the Wizard replied. "Let's start with decentralization. Unlike the current web, which is controlled by a few large companies, Web 3 is decentralized, meaning no single entity has control. Instead, it's powered by a network of users (decentralization)."

With a wave of the Wizard's staff, a shimmering portal opened, leading them into a grand hall filled with creatures interacting and trading directly with each other.

"First, let's explore decentralization," the Wizard said, leading them to a group of foxes and rabbits exchanging goods. "In Web 3, users can interact directly without intermediaries, making the system more transparent and resilient (peer-to-peer)."

Barry watched as the foxes and rabbits traded items seamlessly. "So, everyone has more control and there are no middlemen?"

"Precisely, Barry," the Wizard replied. "Next, let's look at interactivity. Web 3 is highly interactive, allowing users to engage with applications in real-time and participate in decision-making processes (interactivity)."

They moved to another section of the hall where creatures were using various devices to interact with dynamic applications. "Users can contribute to and modify applications directly, creating a more engaging and personalized experience," the Wizard explained.

Robbie hopped around the hall. "What about user control?"

The Wizard smiled. "User control is a fundamental aspect of Web 3. Users have full control over their data and digital assets, deciding how they are used and shared (user control)."

They arrived at a station where a pixie was managing her personal data and assets. "With Web 3, you own your information and can choose exactly how it's used, giving you more privacy and security," the Wizard explained.

Barry saw the pixie granting access to her data selectively. "So, it's like having complete ownership of your digital life?"

"Exactly," the Wizard replied. "Now, let's talk about decentralized applications, or dApps. These are applications that run on a decentralized network rather than a single server (decentralized applications)."

They moved to a platform where various creatures were using different dApps for trading, gaming, and social interactions. "dApps offer the same functionalities as traditional apps but with enhanced security and transparency," the Wizard explained.

Robbie clapped his paws. "That sounds amazing! What else?"

The Wizard nodded. "Another key feature is the blockchain, which is the underlying technology for Web 3. It's a distributed ledger that records all transactions transparently and securely (blockchain)."

They arrived at a display showing a chain of interconnected blocks. "Blockchain ensures that all data is securely recorded and cannot be altered, providing a trustworthy foundation for Web 3," the Wizard explained.

Barry looked fascinated. "What about the money used in Web 3?"

"Ah, yes," the Wizard continued. "Cryptocurrency is the digital currency used within Web 3 to facilitate transactions and reward participants (cryptocurrency). It operates on blockchain technology and enables peer-to-peer financial interactions."

They moved on to a section where creatures were exchanging these digital currencies. "Cryptocurrency ensures secure and direct transactions between users without the need for intermediaries," the Wizard said.

Robbie's eyes widened. "What about these 'smart contracts' I've heard about?"

The Wizard nodded. "Smart contracts are self-executing contracts with the terms directly written into code. They automatically execute transactions when predefined conditions are met, ensuring trust and efficiency (smart contracts)."

They arrived at a table where a rabbit was demonstrating a smart contract in action. "Smart contracts eliminate the need for middlemen and ensure that agreements are honored automatically," the Wizard explained.

Barry and Robbie spent the rest of the day exploring the world of Web 3, amazed by its features and implications. By the time the sun began to set, they felt enlightened and excited about the possibilities.

As they made their way back through the portal, Robbie couldn't help but make Barry laugh with his impressions of the Wise Old Wizard explaining Web 3.

Barry, feeling wiser and more informed, knew that with the knowledge of these technologies, they could explore and innovate in ways they had never imagined.

Explanation of Concepts

1. **Next Generation Internet**: Web 3 is the next iteration of the internet, designed to be more decentralized, interactive, and controlled by users. It leverages new technologies to enhance online experiences and empower individuals.
2. **Decentralization**: Unlike the current web, which is controlled by a few large companies, Web 3 is decentralized. This means no single entity has control, and the network is powered by a community of users who interact directly with each other.
3. **Peer-to-Peer**: In a decentralized system, users can interact directly with each other without intermediaries. This peer-to-peer interaction makes the system more transparent and resilient, reducing reliance on centralized authorities.
4. **Interactivity**: Web 3 is highly interactive, allowing users to engage with applications in real-time and participate in decision-making processes. This creates a more engaging and personalized online experience.
5. **User Control**: Web 3 emphasizes user control, giving individuals full ownership of their data and digital assets. Users decide how their information is used and shared, enhancing privacy and security.
6. **Decentralized Applications (dApps)**: These are applications that run on a decentralized network rather than a single server. dApps offer similar functionalities to traditional apps but with improved security and transparency.

7. **Blockchain**: The underlying technology for Web 3, blockchain is a distributed ledger that records all transactions transparently and securely. It ensures that data cannot be altered, providing a trustworthy foundation for decentralized systems.
8. **Cryptocurrency**: Digital currencies used within the Web 3 ecosystem to facilitate transactions and reward participants. Cryptocurrencies operate on blockchain technology and enable peer-to-peer financial interactions.
9. **Smart Contracts**: Self-executing contracts with the terms directly written into code. Smart contracts automatically execute transactions when predefined conditions are met, ensuring trust and efficiency.
10. **Ownership**: In Web 3, users have full ownership of their digital assets, including data, content, and tokens. This ownership model enhances security and control over personal information.
11. **Tokens**: Digital assets representing various types of value, including utility tokens for accessing services and governance tokens for voting on decisions within a decentralized community.
12. **Distributed Ledger**: A database that is consensually shared and synchronized across multiple sites, institutions, or geographies. Blockchain is a type of distributed ledger used in Web 3 to record transactions securely and transparently.

Questions

1. What is Web 3, and how does it differ from the current web?

    A. Web 3 is the current version of the internet controlled by large companies.

    B. Web 3 is the next generation of the internet, designed to be more decentralized, interactive, and controlled by users.

    C. Web 3 is a social media platform for sharing content.

2. What is decentralization in the context of Web 3?

    A. The process of controlling the web by a single large company.

    B. A system where no single entity has control, and users interact directly with each other.

    C. A method of increasing website traffic.

3. What role does blockchain play in Web 3?

    A. It is used to create social media profiles.

    B. Blockchain is a distributed ledger that records all transactions transparently and securely, providing the foundation for Web 3.

    C. Blockchain is a tool for editing videos.

4. What are smart contracts, and how do they work?

   A. Smart contracts are paper agreements signed by two parties.

   B. Smart contracts are self-executing contracts with terms written into code that automatically execute transactions when conditions are met.

   C. Smart contracts are emails sent to confirm a purchase.

5. Why is user control important in Web 3?

   A. It allows users to rely on companies to manage their data.

   B. It gives users full ownership of their data and digital assets, enhancing privacy and security.

   C. It helps users create more social media posts.

Answers

1. **B** - Web 3 is the next generation of the internet, designed to be more decentralized, interactive, and controlled by users.
2. **B** - Decentralization in Web 3 means no single entity has control, and users interact directly with each other.

3. **B** - Blockchain is a distributed ledger that records all transactions transparently and securely, providing the foundation for Web 3.
4. **B** - Smart contracts are self-executing contracts with terms written into code that automatically execute transactions when conditions are met.
5. **B** - User control is important in Web 3 because it gives users full ownership of their data and digital assets, enhancing privacy and security.

Hashing Insights

A gentle breeze rustled the leaves, carrying the sweet scent of blooming flowers through the forest. A fox glanced up as Robbie Rabbit, donning his ever-present feathered hat, emerged from the underbrush, clutching a scroll tightly. He hopped over to Barry Bear, who was arranging his collection of shiny pebbles with meticulous care.

"Barry! The Wise Old Wizard has sent us on another quest!" Robbie exclaimed, his voice bubbling with enthusiasm.

Barry looked up with a smile. "What's it about this time, Robbie?"

"It's about something called Blockchain and its ledger! We need to learn what they are and how they work!" Robbie said, his eyes twinkling with curiosity.

"Blockchain? That sounds intriguing," Barry replied, setting aside his pebbles.

They made their way to the Wise Old Wizard's tower, where the Wizard greeted them warmly, his eyes sparkling with wisdom.

"Ah, Barry and Robbie, welcome," the Wizard began. "Today, we will explore the concept of Blockchain and its ledger, and understand their significance."

Barry tilted his head. "What is Blockchain, and how does it work?"

The Wizard nodded. "Blockchain is like a magical book that keeps a record of all transactions that happen within a network. Each page of this book is called a block, and they are linked together in a chain, forming the blockchain (magical book of records)."

Robbie's ears perked up. "So, it's like a big, magical ledger?"

"Exactly, Robbie," the Wizard replied. "Let's start with the concept of a ledger. A ledger is a record-keeping system that logs all transactions in an orderly manner (record-keeping system)."

With a wave of the Wizard's staff, a shimmering portal opened, leading them into a grand hall filled with creatures busy recording and verifying transactions.

"First, let's explore how a ledger works," the Wizard said, leading them to a group of foxes and rabbits noting down trades. "In a traditional ledger, entries are recorded by a trusted authority. But in a blockchain, the ledger is maintained by everyone in the network, ensuring transparency and security (shared ledger)."

Barry watched as the foxes and rabbits compared notes to ensure accuracy. "So, everyone helps keep the record honest?"

"Precisely, Barry," the Wizard replied. "Next, let's look at how blocks are created. When a transaction occurs, it is verified by the network and then recorded in a block. Each block contains a list of transactions and a reference to the previous block, forming a chain (block creation)."

They moved to another section of the hall where a rabbit was adding a new block to the chain. "This reference to the previous block ensures that the chain remains unbroken and tamper-proof," the Wizard explained.

Robbie hopped around the hall. "What about the security of these blocks?"

The Wizard smiled. "Each block is secured by a special code called a hash, which is unique to that block. If someone tries to change the information in a block, the hash changes, alerting the network to the tampering (hash for security)."

They arrived at a station where a pixie was demonstrating how a hash works. "Hashes ensure that once a block is added to the chain, it cannot be altered without altering all subsequent blocks, which is nearly impossible," the Wizard explained.

Barry saw the pixie show how changing even a small detail in the block altered its hash. "So, the hash keeps the information safe?"

"Exactly," the Wizard replied. "Now, let's talk about the concept of consensus. In a blockchain network, all participants must agree on the validity of a transaction before it is added to the ledger (consensus)."

They moved to a gathering of creatures discussing and agreeing on the latest transactions. "This agreement ensures that only valid transactions are recorded, maintaining the integrity of the ledger," the Wizard explained.

Robbie clapped his paws. "This is amazing! What else?"

The Wizard nodded. "Finally, let's discuss the decentralization of blockchain. Unlike traditional systems where a central authority controls the ledger, blockchain is decentralized, meaning no single entity has control. This decentralization enhances security and trust (decentralization)."

Barry and Robbie spent the rest of the day exploring the world of blockchain, amazed by its structure, operation, and impact. By the time the sun began to set, they felt enlightened and excited about the possibilities.

As they made their way back through the portal, Robbie couldn't help but make Barry laugh with his impressions of the Wise Old Wizard explaining blockchain.

Barry, feeling wiser and more informed, knew that with the knowledge of these technologies, they could explore and innovate in ways they had never imagined.

Explanation of Concepts

1. **Magical Book of Records**: Blockchain is like a magical book that keeps a record of all transactions that happen within a network. Each page of this book is called a block, and they are linked together in a chain, forming the blockchain.
2. **Record-Keeping System**: A ledger is a record-keeping system that logs all transactions in an orderly manner. In a blockchain, the ledger is maintained by everyone in the network, ensuring transparency and security.
3. **Shared Ledger**: In a traditional ledger, entries are recorded by a trusted authority. But in a blockchain, the ledger is maintained by everyone in the network, ensuring transparency and security.
4. **Block Creation**: When a transaction occurs, it is verified by the network and then recorded in a block. Each block contains a list of transactions and a reference to the previous block, forming a chain.
5. **Hash for Security**: Each block is secured by a special code called a hash, which is unique to that block. If someone tries to change the information in a block, the hash changes, alerting the network to the tampering.
6. **Consensus**: In a blockchain network, all participants must agree on the validity of a transaction before it is added to the ledger. This agreement ensures that only valid transactions are recorded, maintaining the integrity of the ledger.
7. **Decentralization**: Unlike traditional systems where a central authority controls the ledger, blockchain is

decentralized, meaning no single entity has control. This decentralization enhances security and trust.

Questions

1. What is a blockchain compared to in the story, and what does it do?

    A. A magical book that keeps a record of all transactions within a network.

    B. A basket that stores different kinds of fruits.

    C. A map that shows the way through the forest.

2. How is a blockchain ledger different from a traditional ledger?

    A. A blockchain ledger is kept by a central authority.

    B. A blockchain ledger is maintained by everyone in the network, ensuring transparency and security.

    C. A blockchain ledger is written on paper.

3. What is a hash in the context of blockchain, and why is it important?

    A. A type of food that animals eat.

    B. A special code that secures each block and alerts the network if someone tries to change the information.

    C. A tool for digging in the ground.

4. What is the purpose of consensus in a blockchain network?

>   A. To make sure everyone has the same idea.
>
>   B. To ensure all participants agree on the validity of a transaction before it is added to the ledger.
>
>   C. To decide what to have for dinner.

5. What does decentralization mean in the context of blockchain?

>   A. The network is controlled by a single leader.
>
>   B. No single entity has control, and the system is maintained by a network of users.
>
>   C. The network is located in a central building.

Answers

1. **A** - A blockchain is compared to a magical book that keeps a record of all transactions within a network.
2. **B** - A blockchain ledger is maintained by everyone in the network, ensuring transparency and security.

3. **B** - A hash is a special code that secures each block and alerts the network if someone tries to change the information.
4. **B** - The purpose of consensus in a blockchain network is to ensure all participants agree on the validity of a transaction before it is added to the ledger.
5. **B** - Decentralization in blockchain means that no single entity has control, and the system is maintained by a network of users.

Chains of Trust

A colorful kite fluttered high in the sky, its tail weaving intricate patterns as it danced on the breeze. Below, Robbie Rabbit, sporting his feathered hat, emerged from the bushes, holding a scroll with a look of intense concentration. He hurried over to Barry Bear, who was stacking his shiny pebbles in perfect pyramids.

"Barry! The Wise Old Wizard has sent us another quest!" Robbie exclaimed, his voice brimming with excitement.

Barry looked up with a smile. "What's it about this time, Robbie?"

"It's about something called Blockchain and its decentralization! We need to learn what it is and how it works!" Robbie said, his eyes gleaming with curiosity.

"Blockchain? That sounds fascinating," Barry replied, setting aside his pebbles.

They made their way to the Wise Old Wizard's tower, where the Wizard greeted them warmly, his eyes twinkling with wisdom.

"Ah, Barry and Robbie, welcome," the Wizard began. "Today, we will explore the concept of Blockchain and its key feature, decentralization, and understand their significance."

Barry tilted his head. "What is Blockchain, and how does it work?"

The Wizard nodded. "Blockchain is like an enchanted ledger that keeps a record of all transactions that happen within a network. Each page of this ledger is called a block, and they are linked together in a chain, forming the blockchain (enchanted ledger)."

Robbie's ears perked up. "So, it's like a magical book of records?"

"Exactly, Robbie," the Wizard replied. "But what makes it special is its decentralization. Unlike traditional systems controlled by a central authority, blockchain operates on a network of many participants who all share and verify the data (network of participants)."

With a wave of the Wizard's staff, a shimmering portal opened, leading them into a grand hall filled with creatures interacting and verifying transactions.

"First, let's explore how decentralization works," the Wizard said, leading them to a group of foxes and rabbits checking records. "In a decentralized system, every participant in the network has a copy of the ledger. When a transaction occurs, it is verified by multiple participants before being added to the blockchain (verification by participants)."

Barry watched as the foxes and rabbits nodded in agreement and added a new transaction to the chain. "So, everyone helps keep the record honest?"

"Precisely, Barry," the Wizard replied. "This process ensures that the data is accurate and cannot be easily tampered with, as altering one copy would immediately be detected by others (data integrity)."

They moved to another section of the hall where a rabbit was explaining the importance of consensus. "In a decentralized system, all participants must agree on the validity of a transaction before it is added to the ledger. This agreement is known as consensus (agreement on transactions)," the Wizard explained.

Robbie hopped around the hall. "What about security? How is everything kept safe?"

The Wizard smiled. "Each block in the chain is secured with a special code called a hash, which is unique to that block. If someone tries to change the information in a block, the hash changes, alerting the network to the tampering (security with hashes)."

They arrived at a station where a pixie was demonstrating how a hash works. "Hashes ensure that once a block is added to the chain, it cannot be altered without altering all subsequent blocks, which is nearly impossible," the Wizard explained.

Barry saw the pixie show how changing even a small detail in the block altered its hash. "So, the hash keeps the information safe?"

"Exactly," the Wizard replied. "And because the blockchain is decentralized, there is no single point of failure. This makes the system more resilient and trustworthy (resilience of decentralization)."

Robbie clapped his paws. "This is amazing! What else?"

The Wizard nodded. "Finally, let's talk about the transparency of blockchain. Because all transactions are recorded on a shared ledger that is accessible to all participants, everyone can see and verify the data (transparency)."

They moved to a gathering where creatures were discussing and reviewing the latest transactions. "This transparency fosters trust among participants, as they can independently verify the accuracy of the information," the Wizard explained.

Barry and Robbie spent the rest of the day exploring the world of blockchain, amazed by its structure, operation, and impact. By the time the sun began to set, they felt enlightened and excited about the possibilities.

As they made their way back through the portal, Robbie couldn't help but make Barry laugh with his impressions of the Wise Old Wizard explaining blockchain.

Barry, feeling wiser and more informed, knew that with the knowledge of these technologies, they could explore and innovate in ways they had never imagined.

Explanation of Concepts

1. **Enchanted Ledger**: Blockchain is like an enchanted ledger that keeps a record of all transactions within a network. Each page of this ledger is called a block, and they are linked together in a chain, forming the blockchain.
2. **Network of Participants**: Unlike traditional systems controlled by a central authority, blockchain operates on a network of many participants who all share and verify the data. This decentralization ensures that no single entity has control over the entire system.
3. **Verification by Participants**: In a decentralized system, every participant in the network has a copy of the ledger. When a transaction occurs, it is verified by multiple participants before being added to the blockchain, ensuring accuracy and security.
4. **Data Integrity**: Decentralization ensures that data is accurate and cannot be easily tampered with. Altering one copy of the ledger would immediately be detected by others, maintaining the integrity of the information.
5. **Agreement on Transactions**: Consensus is the process by which all participants in a decentralized system agree on the validity of a transaction before it is added to the ledger. This agreement ensures that only valid transactions are recorded.
6. **Security with Hashes**: Each block in the blockchain is secured with a unique code called a hash. If someone tries to change the information in a block, the hash

changes, alerting the network to the tampering. This makes the blockchain secure and tamper-proof.

7. **Resilience of Decentralization**: Because the blockchain is decentralized, there is no single point of failure. This makes the system more resilient and trustworthy, as it can continue to operate even if some participants fail.

8. **Transparency**: All transactions on the blockchain are recorded on a shared ledger that is accessible to all participants. This transparency allows everyone to see and verify the data, fostering trust and accountability within the network.

Questions

1. What is a blockchain compared to in the story, and what does it do?

    A. A magical mirror that shows the future

    B. An enchanted ledger that keeps a record of all transactions within a network

    C. A treasure map that leads to hidden riches

2. How does decentralization work in a blockchain system?

    A. One central authority controls all the data

    B. Everyone in the network shares and verifies the data, ensuring no single entity has control

    C. Only a few selected participants can verify the transactions

3. What is a hash, and why is it important in a blockchain?

    A. A type of password that unlocks the blockchain

    B. A unique code that secures each block and alerts the network if someone tries to tamper with the data

    C. A tool used to build blocks in the chain

4. What does consensus mean in the context of a blockchain?

A. A magical spell that makes everyone agree

B. The process by which all participants agree on the validity of a transaction before it is added to the ledger

C. A vote to decide what to do with the blockchain

5. Why is transparency important in a blockchain network?

    A. It hides all transactions from everyone

    B. It allows everyone to see and verify the data, fostering trust and accountability

    C. It makes the blockchain invisible to outsiders

Answers

1. **B** - A blockchain is compared to an enchanted ledger that keeps a record of all transactions within a network.
2. **B** - In a decentralized blockchain system, everyone in the network shares and verifies the data, ensuring no single entity has control.
3. **B** - A hash is a unique code that secures each block and alerts the network if someone tries to tamper with the data.
4. **B** - Consensus in a blockchain is the process by which all participants agree on the validity of a transaction before it is added to the ledger.

5. **B** - Transparency is important in a blockchain because it allows everyone to see and verify the data, fostering trust and accountability within the network.

Squirrels Solve Puzzles

A squirrel chattering high up in the trees distracted Robbie Rabbit as he emerged from the underbrush, his feathered hat flopping comically as he hopped over to Barry Bear. Robbie clutched a scroll, excitement evident in his every movement.

"Barry! The Wise Old Wizard has sent us another quest!" Robbie exclaimed, practically bouncing with enthusiasm.

Barry looked up with a smile. "What's it about this time, Robbie?"

"It's about something called Blockchain, specifically nodes, miners, and consensus! We need to learn what they are and how they work!" Robbie said, his eyes twinkling with curiosity.

"Blockchain? That sounds fascinating," Barry replied, setting aside his pebbles.

They made their way to the Wise Old Wizard's tower, where the Wizard greeted them warmly, his eyes sparkling with wisdom.

"Ah, Barry and Robbie, welcome," the Wizard began. "Today, we will explore the concepts of Blockchain, focusing on nodes, miners, and consensus, and understand their significance."

Barry tilted his head. "What are nodes, miners, and consensus, and how do they work?"

The Wizard nodded. "Imagine a vast network of enchanted trees, each with its own role. A node is like a tree that stores all the information about the forest, a miner is like a diligent squirrel gathering acorns to solve puzzles, and consensus is the agreement among all the creatures about the state of the forest (nodes, miners, consensus)."

Robbie's ears perked up. "So, it's like a magical network?"

"Exactly, Robbie," the Wizard replied. "Let's start with nodes. In the blockchain, nodes are computers that store and maintain the ledger, ensuring that all data is accurate and up-to-date (nodes)."

With a wave of the Wizard's staff, a shimmering portal opened, leading them into a grand hall filled with creatures interacting and verifying information.

"First, let's explore how nodes work," the Wizard said, leading them to a group of foxes and rabbits checking records. "Nodes store the entire history of transactions in the blockchain. They communicate with each other to share information and keep everything synchronized (information storage)."

Barry watched as the foxes and rabbits nodded in agreement and updated their records. "So, nodes make sure everyone has the same information?"

"Precisely, Barry," the Wizard replied. "Next, let's look at miners. In the blockchain, miners are special nodes that perform the important task of validating transactions and adding them to the blockchain (miners)."

They moved to another section of the hall where a group of squirrels were solving complex puzzles. "Miners solve mathematical problems to validate transactions. The first miner to solve the problem gets to add the block to the chain and is rewarded for their effort (transaction validation)," the Wizard explained.

Robbie hopped around the hall. "What about consensus? How do all the nodes agree on the same information?"

The Wizard smiled. "Consensus is the process by which all nodes agree on the validity of transactions. This ensures that the blockchain remains accurate and trustworthy (agreement on validity)."

They arrived at a station where a pixie was demonstrating the consensus process. "There are different methods to achieve consensus, but one common method is called proof-of-work, where miners compete to solve puzzles. Once a block is added, all nodes update their records to reflect the new information (proof-of-work)."

Barry saw the pixie show how nodes communicated and reached an agreement. "So, consensus makes sure everyone agrees on the same data?"

"Exactly," the Wizard replied. "This ensures that the blockchain is secure and reliable, as all nodes work together to maintain its integrity (security and reliability)."

Robbie clapped his paws. "This is amazing! What else?"

The Wizard nodded. "Let's talk about the benefits of decentralization. Because the blockchain is maintained by many nodes, it is not controlled by a single entity. This makes it more secure and less prone to failure (decentralization)."

Barry and Robbie spent the rest of the day exploring the world of blockchain, amazed by its structure, operation, and impact. By the time the sun began to set, they felt enlightened and excited about the possibilities.

As they made their way back through the portal, Robbie couldn't help but make Barry laugh with his impressions of the Wise Old Wizard explaining blockchain.

Barry, feeling wiser and more informed, knew that with the knowledge of these technologies, they could explore and innovate in ways they had never imagined.

Explanation of Concepts

1. **Nodes**: In the blockchain, nodes are computers that store and maintain the ledger. They ensure that all data is accurate and up-to-date, communicating with each other to share information and keep everything synchronized.
2. **Information Storage**: Nodes store the entire history of transactions in the blockchain. They communicate to ensure that everyone has the same, accurate information, maintaining the integrity of the blockchain.
3. **Miners**: Miners are special nodes that perform the task of validating transactions and adding them to the blockchain. They solve complex mathematical problems, and the first to solve the problem gets to add the block to the chain and is rewarded.
4. **Transaction Validation**: Miners solve mathematical problems to validate transactions. Once a problem is solved, the validated transactions are added to the blockchain, and the miner is rewarded for their effort.
5. **Consensus**: Consensus is the process by which all nodes agree on the validity of transactions. This ensures that the blockchain remains accurate and trustworthy, as all nodes work together to maintain its integrity.
6. **Agreement on Validity**: Consensus methods, like proof-of-work, require miners to solve puzzles. Once a block is added, all nodes update their records, ensuring that everyone agrees on the same data.
7. **Security and Reliability**: Consensus ensures that the blockchain is secure and reliable. Nodes work together

to maintain the accuracy and integrity of the blockchain, preventing tampering and fraud.
8. **Decentralization**: The blockchain is maintained by many nodes, making it decentralized. This means it is not controlled by a single entity, enhancing its security and reducing the risk of failure.

Questions

1. What role do nodes play in a blockchain?

    A. They control all the transactions

    B. They store and maintain the ledger, ensuring that all data is accurate and up-to-date

    C. They are responsible for solving puzzles to add blocks

2. What task do miners perform in the blockchain?

    A. They store the entire history of transactions

    B. They solve mathematical problems to validate transactions and add them to the blockchain

    C. They create new blocks without any verification process

3. How do nodes ensure that everyone in the network has the same, accurate information?

    A. By guessing the information

    B. By communicating and sharing information to keep everything synchronized

    C. By following the instructions of a central authority

4. What is consensus in the context of blockchain?

A. A method to randomly select a node for adding new blocks

B. The process by which all nodes agree on the validity of transactions, ensuring the blockchain's accuracy and trustworthiness

C. A way for miners to compete without solving any puzzles

5. Why is decentralization important in a blockchain?

    A. It makes the blockchain controlled by a single entity

    B. It enhances the security and reliability of the blockchain by ensuring it is maintained by many nodes rather than a central authority

    C. It slows down the blockchain's operation by spreading tasks among too many participants

Answers

1. **B** - Nodes store and maintain the ledger, ensuring that all data is accurate and up-to-date.

2. **B** - Miners solve mathematical problems to validate transactions and add them to the blockchain.
3. **B** - Nodes ensure that everyone in the network has the same, accurate information by communicating and sharing information to keep everything synchronized.
4. **B** - Consensus is the process by which all nodes agree on the validity of transactions, ensuring the blockchain's accuracy and trustworthiness.
5. **B** - Decentralization enhances the security and reliability of the blockchain by ensuring it is maintained by many nodes rather than a central authority.

Blocks of Wisdom

A flock of birds erupted from the treetops, their wings fluttering in perfect harmony, captivating Robbie Rabbit, whose feathered hat bobbed with every enthusiastic hop. Clutching a scroll in one paw, his excitement was palpable, as if he could scarcely wait to unveil its secrets. Robbie's gaze landed on Barry Bear, who meticulously arranged his collection of shiny pebbles into intricate patterns on the forest floor.

"Barry! The Wise Old Wizard has sent us another quest!" Robbie exclaimed, his voice brimming with excitement.

Barry looked up with a smile. "What's it about this time, Robbie?"

"It's about something called Blockchain, specifically hashing and blocks! We need to learn what they are and how they work!" Robbie said, his eyes gleaming with curiosity.

"Blockchain? That sounds fascinating," Barry replied, setting aside his pebbles.

They made their way to the Wise Old Wizard's tower, where the Wizard greeted them warmly, his eyes twinkling with wisdom.

"Ah, Barry and Robbie, welcome," the Wizard began. "Today, we will explore the concepts of Blockchain, focusing on hashing and blocks, and understand their significance."

Barry tilted his head. "What are hashing and blocks, and how do they work?"

The Wizard nodded. "Imagine a magical book that records everything that happens in the forest. Each page of this book is called a block, and to keep the pages in order and secure, we use a special spell called hashing (magical book, block, hashing)."

Robbie's ears perked up. "So, it's like a secure way to keep track of everything?"

"Exactly, Robbie," the Wizard replied. "Let's start with blocks. A block is a collection of records, like a page in our magical book, that contains information about various transactions or events that have occurred (block)."

With a wave of the Wizard's staff, a shimmering portal opened, leading them into a grand hall filled with creatures busy recording and verifying transactions.

"First, let's explore how blocks work," the Wizard said, leading them to a group of foxes and rabbits reviewing records. "Each block contains a list of transactions, and a unique identifier called a hash, which helps keep everything in order and secure (unique identifier)."

Barry watched as the foxes and rabbits checked each record and added them to a block. "So, blocks keep everything organized and secure?"

"Precisely, Barry," the Wizard replied. "Next, let's look at hashing. Hashing is like a magical spell that takes all the information in a block and transforms it into a unique string of characters, which is the hash (hashing)."

They moved to another section of the hall where a group of pixies were demonstrating the hashing process. "Hashing ensures that each block is unique and cannot be tampered with. If anyone tries to change the information in a block, the hash will change, alerting everyone to the tampering (tamper detection)."

Robbie hopped around the hall. "What about linking the blocks together?"

The Wizard smiled. "That's where the magic of blockchain comes in. Each block not only contains its own hash but also the hash of the previous block, linking them together in a chain. This makes the blockchain secure and immutable (chain linking)."

They arrived at a station where a rabbit was adding a new block to the chain. "By including the hash of the previous block, any changes to a block will break the chain, making it obvious that tampering has occurred (immutability)," the Wizard explained.

Barry saw the rabbit show how altering a block's data changed its hash and broke the chain. "So, the chain of hashes keeps everything secure?"

"Exactly," the Wizard replied. "Now, let's talk about why this is important. Blockchain's structure and hashing provide a reliable way to record and verify transactions without needing a central authority, making the system decentralized and trustworthy (decentralization)."

Barry and Robbie spent the rest of the day exploring the world of blockchain, amazed by its structure, operation, and impact. By the time the sun began to set, they felt enlightened and excited about the possibilities.

As they made their way back through the portal, Robbie couldn't help but make Barry laugh with his impressions of the Wise Old Wizard explaining blockchain.

Barry, feeling wiser and more informed, knew that with the knowledge of these technologies, they could explore and innovate in ways they had never imagined.

Explanation of Concepts

1. **Magical Book**: Blockchain is like a magical book that records all transactions within a network. Each page of this book is called a block, and they are linked together in a chain.
2. **Block**: A block is a collection of records, like a page in a book, that contains information about various transactions or events. Each block has a unique identifier called a hash, which helps keep everything in order and secure.
3. **Unique Identifier**: Each block contains a list of transactions and a hash. The hash is a unique string of characters that identifies the block and ensures its integrity.
4. **Hashing**: Hashing is the process of transforming all the information in a block into a unique string of characters, the hash. This ensures that each block is unique and tamper-proof.
5. **Tamper Detection**: Hashing ensures that any attempt to change the information in a block will change its hash, alerting everyone to the tampering.
6. **Chain Linking**: Each block contains its own hash and the hash of the previous block, linking them together in a chain. This makes the blockchain secure and immutable.
7. **Immutability**: By including the hash of the previous block, any changes to a block will break the chain, making it obvious that tampering has occurred. This ensures the integrity of the blockchain.

8. **Decentralization**: Blockchain's structure and hashing provide a reliable way to record and verify transactions without needing a central authority, making the system decentralized and trustworthy.

Questions

1. What is a block in the context of a blockchain?

    A. A physical book

    B. A collection of records or transactions with a unique identifier

    C. A single transaction in the blockchain

2. What role does hashing play in a blockchain?

    A. It organizes the transactions alphabetically

    B. It transforms the information in a block into a unique string of characters, ensuring security and integrity

    C. It duplicates the transactions in the blockchain

3. How does blockchain detect if someone has tampered with a block?

    A. By checking the color of the block

    B. By noticing that the hash of the block has changed, which would alert everyone to the tampering

    C. By removing the block from the chain

4. What happens when a block is linked to the previous block's hash?

A. The blocks become more colorful

B. The blocks are securely connected, forming a chain that ensures immutability

C. The previous block is deleted

5. Why is decentralization important in a blockchain?

    A. It allows one central authority to control all the data

    B. It provides a reliable way to record and verify transactions without needing a central authority, making the system trustworthy

    C. It makes the blockchain slower and less efficient

Answers

1. **B** - A block is a collection of records or transactions with a unique identifier.
2. **B** - Hashing transforms the information in a block into a unique string of characters, ensuring security and integrity.
3. **B** - Blockchain detects tampering by noticing that the hash of the block has changed, which would alert everyone to the tampering.

4. **B** - When a block is linked to the previous block's hash, the blocks are securely connected, forming a chain that ensures immutability.
5. **B** - Decentralization provides a reliable way to record and verify transactions without needing a central authority, making the system trustworthy.

Self-Executing Scrolls

A gust of wind swept through the clearing, rustling the leaves and sending a flurry of dandelion seeds into the air. Robbie Rabbit, with his feathered hat askew, hopped over excitedly to Barry Bear, who was arranging his shiny pebbles in a perfect circle.

"Barry! The Wise Old Wizard has sent us another quest!" Robbie exclaimed, practically bouncing with anticipation.

Barry looked up with a smile. "What's it about this time, Robbie?"

"It's about something called Blockchain, specifically smart contracts! We need to learn what they are and how they work!" Robbie said, his eyes twinkling with curiosity.

"Smart contracts? That sounds intriguing," Barry replied, setting aside his pebbles.

They made their way to the Wise Old Wizard's tower, where the Wizard greeted them warmly, his eyes sparkling with wisdom.

"Ah, Barry and Robbie, welcome," the Wizard began. "Today, we will explore the concept of Blockchain, focusing on smart contracts, and understand their significance."

Barry tilted his head. "What are smart contracts, and how do they work?"

The Wizard nodded. "Imagine a magical scroll that enforces the terms of an agreement automatically, without the need for a middleman. That's what a smart contract does (automated agreement)."

Robbie's ears perked up. "So, it's like an enchanted contract that works by itself?"

"Exactly, Robbie," the Wizard replied. "Let's start with the basics. A smart contract is a self-executing contract with the terms of the agreement directly written into code. It automatically executes and enforces the terms when predefined conditions are met (self-executing contract)."

With a wave of the Wizard's staff, a shimmering portal opened, leading them into a grand hall filled with creatures interacting and trading seamlessly.

"First, let's explore how smart contracts work," the Wizard said, leading them to a group of foxes and rabbits making trades. "When the conditions of the contract are met, the smart contract automatically executes the agreed-upon actions without any human intervention (automatic execution)."

Barry watched as the foxes and rabbits completed their trades effortlessly. "So, smart contracts do everything on their own?"

"Precisely, Barry," the Wizard replied. "Next, let's look at how they ensure trust. Because smart contracts are stored on the blockchain, they are transparent and immutable. This means everyone can see the contract terms, and no one can alter them once they are set (transparency and immutability)."

They moved to another section of the hall where a group of pixies were demonstrating how smart contracts worked on the blockchain. "The transparency of the blockchain ensures that all parties can trust the contract, knowing that it will be executed as agreed (trust and reliability)."

Robbie hopped around the hall. "What about security? How are smart contracts kept safe?"

The Wizard smiled. "Smart contracts are secured by the blockchain's technology, which makes them resistant to tampering and fraud. The decentralized nature of the blockchain means there is no single point of failure (security)."

They arrived at a station where a rabbit was explaining the security features of smart contracts. "Because smart contracts are part of the blockchain, they inherit its security features, making them highly reliable and secure (inheritance of security)."

Barry saw the rabbit show how altering the contract was impossible without changing the entire blockchain. "So, the blockchain keeps the contracts safe?"

"Exactly," the Wizard replied. "Now, let's talk about the benefits. Smart contracts can be used for a variety of applications, from simple trades to complex agreements, reducing the need for intermediaries and lowering costs (applications and benefits)."

Barry and Robbie spent the rest of the day exploring the world of smart contracts, amazed by their structure, operation, and impact. By the time the sun began to set, they felt enlightened and excited about the possibilities.

As they made their way back through the portal, Robbie couldn't help but make Barry laugh with his impressions of the Wise Old Wizard explaining smart contracts.

Barry, feeling wiser and more informed, knew that with the knowledge of these technologies, they could explore and innovate in ways they had never imagined.

Explanation of Concepts

1. **Automated Agreement**: A smart contract is like a magical scroll that enforces the terms of an agreement automatically, without the need for a middleman. It ensures that the terms are met and actions are executed automatically.
2. **Self-Executing Contract**: A smart contract is a self-executing contract with the terms of the agreement directly written into code. It automatically executes and enforces the terms when predefined conditions are met.
3. **Automatic Execution**: When the conditions of the contract are met, the smart contract automatically executes the agreed-upon actions without any human intervention. This ensures that the contract is carried out as intended.
4. **Transparency and Immutability**: Smart contracts are stored on the blockchain, making them transparent and immutable. This means everyone can see the contract terms, and no one can alter them once they are set, ensuring trust and reliability.
5. **Trust and Reliability**: The transparency of the blockchain ensures that all parties can trust the contract, knowing that it will be executed as agreed. This reliability is a key feature of smart contracts.
6. **Security**: Smart contracts are secured by the blockchain's technology, which makes them resistant to tampering and fraud. The decentralized nature of the blockchain means there is no single point of failure, enhancing security.

7. **Inheritance of Security**: Because smart contracts are part of the blockchain, they inherit its security features, making them highly reliable and secure. This ensures that the contracts cannot be altered or tampered with.
8. **Applications and Benefits**: Smart contracts can be used for a variety of applications, from simple trades to complex agreements, reducing the need for intermediaries and lowering costs. This versatility makes them a powerful tool in many different scenarios.

Questions

1. What is a smart contract, and how does it function?

    A. A written agreement between two parties that requires a notary

    B. A self-executing contract with terms written into code that automatically executes when conditions are met

    C. A verbal agreement between friends

2. What makes smart contracts secure and trustworthy?

    A. They are stored in a safe place

    B. They are stored on the blockchain, making them transparent and immutable

    C. They are kept secret from everyone

3. How do smart contracts ensure that terms are met without human intervention?

    A. By requiring a manager to oversee the contract

    B. By automatically executing actions when predefined conditions are met

    C. By asking all parties to manually approve each step

4. Why is it impossible to alter a smart contract once it is set?

A. Because it is locked in a safe

B. Because it is written in permanent ink

C. Because it is stored on the blockchain, making it immutable and secure from tampering

5. What are some benefits of using smart contracts?

   A. They require many intermediaries

   B. They reduce the need for intermediaries, lower costs, and can be used for various applications

   C. They are complicated and hard to understand

Answers

1. **B** - A smart contract is a self-executing contract with terms written into code that automatically executes when conditions are met.
2. **B** - Smart contracts are stored on the blockchain, making them transparent and immutable.
3. **B** - Smart contracts automatically execute actions when predefined conditions are met, ensuring terms are met without human intervention.
4. **C** - It is impossible to alter a smart contract once it is set because it is stored on the blockchain, making it immutable and secure from tampering.

5. **B** - Smart contracts reduce the need for intermediaries, lower costs, and can be used for various applications.

Forked Paths Ahead

A sudden squawk from a blue jay startled the forest creatures, sending a ripple of whispers through the underbrush. Robbie Rabbit, sporting his ever-present feathered hat, emerged from behind a tree, clutching a scroll with great excitement. He hopped over to Barry Bear and his grumpy cousin, Garry Bear, who were busy sorting through a pile of berries.

"Barry! Garry! The Wise Old Wizard has sent us another quest!" Robbie exclaimed, practically bouncing with anticipation.

Garry grumbled, "I hope it's something interesting this time."

Barry smiled. "What's it about, Robbie?"

"It's about something called Blockchain, specifically forks and immutability! We need to learn what they are and how they work!" Robbie said, his eyes twinkling with curiosity.

"Blockchain? Sounds fascinating," Barry replied.

They made their way to the Wise Old Wizard's tower, where the Wizard greeted them warmly, his eyes sparkling with wisdom.

"Ah, Barry, Robbie, and Garry, welcome," the Wizard began. "Today, we will explore the concepts of Blockchain, focusing on forks and immutability, and understand their significance."

Garry crossed his arms. "Forks and immutability? Sounds complicated."

The Wizard chuckled. "Not at all, Garry. Let's start with the basics. Imagine a magical book that records everything that happens in the forest. Each page is called a block, and they are linked together in a chain, forming the blockchain (magical book, block, chain)."

Robbie's ears perked up. "So, what are forks?"

"Excellent question, Robbie," the Wizard replied. "A fork occurs when there is a disagreement among the participants about the next page of the book. This disagreement creates two separate paths, or forks, in the chain, each representing a different version of events (disagreement, separate paths)."

With a wave of the Wizard's staff, a shimmering portal opened, leading them into a grand hall filled with creatures arguing over which path to take.

"First, let's explore how forks work," the Wizard said, leading them to a group of foxes and rabbits debating. "When the community cannot agree on the next block, the chain splits into two, creating a fork. Each side follows its own path until a consensus is reached (split chain, consensus)."

Barry watched as the foxes and rabbits eventually agreed on a single path, rejoining the chain. "So, forks can be resolved?"

"Precisely, Barry," the Wizard replied. "Now, let's talk about immutability. Once a block is added to the blockchain, it cannot be changed or deleted. This makes the blockchain immutable, ensuring that all records are permanent and tamper-proof (unchangeable, permanent)."

Garry's frown deepened. "Why is immutability so important?"

The Wizard smiled. "Immutability ensures the integrity and trustworthiness of the blockchain. Because the records cannot be altered, everyone can trust that the information is accurate and secure (integrity, trustworthiness)."

They moved to another section of the hall where a group of pixies were demonstrating the immutability of the blocks. "Each block contains a unique code, called a hash, which links it to the previous block. If someone tries to change a block, the hash changes, breaking the chain and alerting everyone to the tampering (unique code, tamper detection)."

Robbie hopped around the hall. "What happens if someone tries to change a block?"

The Wizard pointed to a pixie showing how altering a block's data changed its hash and broke the chain. "If a block is tampered with, it will no longer match the rest of the chain, making it easy to detect and prevent fraud (tamper prevention)."

Barry saw the pixie show how the unchanged blocks remained secure. "So, the chain of hashes keeps everything safe?"

"Exactly," the Wizard replied. "Now, let's talk about the benefits of forks and immutability. Forks allow for flexibility and innovation in the blockchain, as they enable the community to explore different paths and solutions. Immutability ensures that the records are secure and trustworthy, making the blockchain a reliable source of truth (flexibility, innovation, reliability)."

Barry and Robbie spent the rest of the day exploring the world of blockchain, amazed by its structure, operation, and impact. Even Garry began to show interest, asking questions and engaging with the demonstrations. By the time the sun began to set, they felt enlightened and excited about the possibilities.

As they made their way back through the portal, Robbie couldn't help but make Barry and Garry laugh with his impressions of the Wise Old Wizard explaining blockchain.

Barry, feeling wiser and more informed, knew that with the knowledge of these technologies, they could explore and innovate in ways they had never imagined.

Explanation of Concepts

1. **Magical Book**: Blockchain is like a magical book that records all transactions within a network. Each page of this book is called a block, and they are linked together in a chain.
2. **Disagreement, Separate Paths**: A fork occurs when there is a disagreement among the participants about the next block in the chain. This creates two separate paths, or forks, each representing a different version of events.
3. **Split Chain, Consensus**: When the community cannot agree on the next block, the chain splits into two, creating a fork. Each side follows its own path until a consensus is reached, and the chain can rejoin as one.
4. **Unchangeable, Permanent**: Immutability means that once a block is added to the blockchain, it cannot be changed or deleted. This ensures that all records are permanent and tamper-proof.
5. **Integrity, Trustworthiness**: Immutability ensures the integrity and trustworthiness of the blockchain. Because the records cannot be altered, everyone can trust that the information is accurate and secure.
6. **Unique Code, Tamper Detection**: Each block contains a unique code, called a hash, which links it to the previous block. If someone tries to change a block, the hash changes, breaking the chain and alerting everyone to the tampering.
7. **Tamper Prevention**: If a block is tampered with, it will no longer match the rest of the chain, making it easy to

detect and prevent fraud. This ensures the security of the blockchain.
8. **Flexibility, Innovation, Reliability**: Forks allow for flexibility and innovation in the blockchain, enabling the community to explore different paths and solutions. Immutability ensures that the records are secure and trustworthy, making the blockchain a reliable source of truth.

Questions

1. What happens when there is a disagreement among participants about the next block in the blockchain?

    A. The chain continues as normal

    B. The chain splits into two separate paths, creating a fork

    C. The blockchain stops working

2. What is immutability in the context of blockchain?

    A. The ability to easily change or delete records

    B. The characteristic that ensures once a block is added, it cannot be changed or deleted

    C. A temporary state that can be altered later

3. Why is immutability important for the blockchain?

    A. It allows everyone to edit the information freely

    B. It ensures the records are permanent, secure, and trustworthy

    C. It makes the blockchain more complicated

4. What does each block in the blockchain contain that links it to the previous block?

    A. A timestamp

    B. A unique code called a hash

C. A list of participants

5. What are some benefits of forks in the blockchain?

    A. They create confusion and instability

    B. They allow for flexibility, innovation, and the exploration of different solutions

    C. They make the blockchain slower

Answers

1. **B** - When there is a disagreement among participants about the next block in the blockchain, the chain splits into two separate paths, creating a fork.
2. **B** - Immutability means that once a block is added to the blockchain, it cannot be changed or deleted.
3. **B** - Immutability is important because it ensures that the records are permanent, secure, and trustworthy.
4. **B** - Each block in the blockchain contains a unique code called a hash that links it to the previous block.
5. **B** - Forks allow for flexibility, innovation, and the exploration of different solutions in the blockchain.

Mining for Knowledge

A loud splash echoed through the forest as a fish leapt out of the river, catching the attention of Robbie Rabbit, who was hopping nearby with his feathered hat perched jauntily on his head. He clutched a scroll in one paw, brimming with excitement. He hurried over to Barry Bear, who was arranging his shiny pebbles, and Kylie Kangaroo, who was practicing her hopping.

"Barry! Kylie! The Wise Old Wizard has sent us on another quest!" Robbie exclaimed, practically bouncing with anticipation.

Kylie tilted her head. "What's it about this time, Robbie?"

"It's about something called Bitcoin! We need to learn what it is and how it works!" Robbie said, his eyes twinkling with curiosity.

"Bitcoin? That sounds fascinating," Barry replied, setting aside his pebbles.

They made their way to the Wise Old Wizard's tower, where the Wizard greeted them warmly, his eyes sparkling with wisdom.

"Ah, Barry, Robbie, and Kylie, welcome," the Wizard began. "Today, we will explore the concept of Bitcoin and understand its significance."

Kylie hopped in place. "What is Bitcoin, and how does it work?"

The Wizard nodded. "Imagine a special kind of coin that only exists in the digital world. It can be used to buy things, send money to others, or even save for the future. That's what Bitcoin is (digital coin)."

Robbie's ears perked up. "So, it's like magic money?"

"Exactly, Robbie," the Wizard replied. "Let's start with how Bitcoin works. Bitcoin is a type of cryptocurrency, which means it uses cryptographic techniques to secure transactions and control the creation of new units (cryptographic techniques)."

With a wave of the Wizard's staff, a shimmering portal opened, leading them into a grand hall filled with creatures trading and exchanging shiny, glowing coins.

"First, let's explore how Bitcoin transactions work," the Wizard said, leading them to a group of foxes and rabbits exchanging coins. "When you send Bitcoin to someone, the transaction is recorded in a public ledger called the blockchain, which keeps track of all the transactions (public ledger)."

Barry watched as the foxes and rabbits completed their trades effortlessly. "So, everyone can see the transactions?"

"Precisely, Barry," the Wizard replied. "Next, let's talk about how new Bitcoins are created. This process is called mining, where powerful computers solve complex puzzles to add new blocks to the blockchain and are rewarded with new Bitcoins (mining)."

They moved to another section of the hall where a group of squirrels were solving puzzles on glowing screens. "Mining ensures that new Bitcoins are created in a controlled manner, and it also helps secure the network by verifying transactions (controlled creation)."

Robbie hopped around the hall. "What makes Bitcoin valuable?"

The Wizard smiled. "Bitcoin's value comes from its limited supply, usefulness, and the trust people have in it. Only a fixed number of Bitcoins will ever be created, making it scarce like gold (limited supply)."

They arrived at a station where a rabbit was explaining the benefits of Bitcoin. "Because Bitcoin can be used anywhere in the world and is not controlled by any government or bank, it offers financial freedom and privacy to its users (financial freedom)."

Barry saw the rabbit show how Bitcoin transactions were fast and efficient. "So, Bitcoin is like a special kind of money that everyone trusts?"

"Exactly," the Wizard replied. "Now, let's talk about the security of Bitcoin. Each Bitcoin transaction is secured by cryptographic techniques, making it nearly impossible to counterfeit or double-spend (transaction security)."

Robbie clapped his paws. "This is amazing! What else?"

The Wizard nodded. "Let's discuss how Bitcoin is stored. Bitcoins are kept in digital wallets, which can be on your computer, phone, or even on special hardware devices. These wallets use private keys to keep your Bitcoins safe (digital wallets)."

Barry and Robbie spent the rest of the day exploring the world of Bitcoin, amazed by its structure, operation, and impact. Even Kylie began to show interest, asking questions and engaging with the demonstrations. By the time the sun began to set, they felt enlightened and excited about the possibilities.

As they made their way back through the portal, Robbie couldn't help but make Barry and Kylie laugh with his impressions of the Wise Old Wizard explaining Bitcoin.

Barry, feeling wiser and more informed, knew that with the knowledge of these technologies, they could explore and innovate in ways they had never imagined.

Explanation of Concepts

1. **Digital Coin**: Bitcoin is a special kind of coin that exists only in the digital world. It can be used to buy things, send money to others, or save for the future. It is not a physical coin but a digital asset.
2. **Cryptographic Techniques**: Bitcoin uses cryptographic techniques to secure transactions and control the creation of new units. This ensures that all transactions are secure and verifiable.
3. **Public Ledger**: When you send Bitcoin to someone, the transaction is recorded in a public ledger called the blockchain. The blockchain keeps track of all transactions, ensuring transparency and security.
4. **Mining**: Mining is the process by which new Bitcoins are created. Powerful computers solve complex puzzles to add new blocks to the blockchain and are rewarded with new Bitcoins. This process secures the network and verifies transactions.
5. **Controlled Creation**: Mining ensures that new Bitcoins are created in a controlled manner. It also helps secure the network by verifying transactions and preventing fraud.
6. **Limited Supply**: Bitcoin's value comes from its limited supply. Only a fixed number of Bitcoins will ever be created, making it scarce like gold. This scarcity contributes to its value.
7. **Financial Freedom**: Bitcoin offers financial freedom and privacy to its users because it can be used anywhere

in the world and is not controlled by any government or bank.

8. **Transaction Security**: Each Bitcoin transaction is secured by cryptographic techniques, making it nearly impossible to counterfeit or double-spend. This ensures the integrity of the currency.
9. **Digital Wallets**: Bitcoins are stored in digital wallets, which can be on your computer, phone, or special hardware devices. These wallets use private keys to keep your Bitcoins safe and secure from unauthorized access.

Questions

1. What is Bitcoin and how does it exist?

    A. A physical coin you can hold in your hand

    B. A special kind of coin that only exists in the digital world

    C. A type of paper currency

2. How are new Bitcoins created?

    A. By printing them in a factory

    B. Through a process called mining, where computers solve puzzles

    C. By finding them hidden in the forest

3. What is the purpose of the public ledger, also known as the blockchain, in Bitcoin transactions?

    A. To keep the coins shiny and new

    B. To record and keep track of all Bitcoin transactions for transparency and security

    C. To hide all transactions from everyone

4. Why is Bitcoin considered valuable?

    A. Because there is an unlimited supply of it

    B. Because it can be easily created by anyone

C. Because it has a limited supply, is useful, and people trust it

5. Where are Bitcoins stored, and how are they kept safe?

    A. In a treasure chest guarded by a dragon

    B. In digital wallets that use private keys to ensure security

    C. Under your pillow

Answers

1. **B** - Bitcoin is a special kind of coin that only exists in the digital world.
2. **B** - New Bitcoins are created through a process called mining, where computers solve puzzles.
3. **B** - The public ledger, or blockchain, records and keeps track of all Bitcoin transactions for transparency and security.
4. **C** - Bitcoin is valuable because it has a limited supply, is useful, and people trust it.
5. **B** - Bitcoins are stored in digital wallets that use private keys to ensure security.

Enlightened by Ethereum

The golden leaves of autumn fluttered down from the trees, casting a warm glow over the forest. Robbie Rabbit, with his feathered hat bouncing, emerged from the bushes holding a scroll. He hurried over to Barry Bear and Kylie Kangaroo, who were playing a game of hopscotch.

"Barry! Kylie! The Wise Old Wizard has sent us on another quest!" Robbie exclaimed, his excitement barely contained.

Kylie tilted her head. "What's it about this time, Robbie?"

"It's about something called Ethereum! We need to learn what it is and how it works!" Robbie said, his eyes shining with curiosity.

"Ethereum? That sounds fascinating," Barry replied, setting aside his game.

They made their way to the Wise Old Wizard's tower, where the Wizard greeted them warmly, his eyes twinkling with wisdom.

"Ah, Barry, Robbie, and Kylie, welcome," the Wizard began. "Today, we will explore the concept of Ethereum and understand its significance."

Kylie hopped in place. "What is Ethereum, and how does it work?"

The Wizard nodded. "Imagine a magical kingdom where not only can you exchange coins, but you can also create and run enchanted spells that perform various tasks automatically. That's what Ethereum is like (magical kingdom with spells)."

Robbie's ears perked up. "So, it's more than just magic money?"

"Exactly, Robbie," the Wizard replied. "Ethereum is a type of cryptocurrency, but it also allows for the creation and execution of smart contracts and decentralized applications, which are like automated spells and tools (automated spells and tools)."

With a wave of the Wizard's staff, a shimmering portal opened, leading them into a grand hall filled with creatures using various magical devices.

"First, let's explore smart contracts," the Wizard said, leading them to a group of foxes and rabbits using enchanted scrolls. "A smart contract is a self-executing agreement with the terms directly written into code. It automatically enforces the terms when conditions are met (self-executing agreement)."

Barry watched as the foxes and rabbits completed tasks effortlessly. "So, smart contracts do everything on their own?"

"Precisely, Barry," the Wizard replied. "Next, let's talk about decentralized applications, or dApps. These are applications that run on the Ethereum network and can perform a wide range of functions without needing a central authority (decentralized applications)."

They moved to another section of the hall where creatures were using various dApps for trading, gaming, and even learning. "dApps offer the same functionalities as traditional apps but with enhanced security and transparency," the Wizard explained.

Robbie hopped around the hall. "What about the magic coins? How are they used?"

The Wizard smiled. "The coins used in Ethereum are called Ether. They are used to pay for transactions, execute smart contracts, and incentivize participants who help maintain the network (incentive coins)."

They arrived at a station where a rabbit was demonstrating how Ether was used to power a dApp. "Ether ensures that the network runs smoothly and that resources are allocated efficiently," the Wizard explained.

Barry saw the rabbit show how transactions were processed quickly and securely. "So, Ether is like the fuel for the magical kingdom?"

"Exactly," the Wizard replied. "Now, let's talk about the benefits of Ethereum. Its flexibility allows developers to create innovative solutions and its decentralized nature ensures that applications are secure and free from censorship (flexibility and security)."

Robbie clapped his paws. "This is amazing! What else?"

The Wizard nodded. "Ethereum also supports token creation, allowing anyone to create their own digital assets that can represent anything from currency to ownership rights (token creation)."

Barry and Robbie spent the rest of the day exploring the world of Ethereum, amazed by its structure, operation, and impact. Even Kylie began to show interest, asking questions and engaging with the demonstrations. By the time the sun began to set, they felt enlightened and excited about the possibilities.

As they made their way back through the portal, Robbie couldn't help but make Barry and Kylie laugh with his impressions of the Wise Old Wizard explaining Ethereum.

Barry, feeling wiser and more informed, knew that with the knowledge of these technologies, they could explore and innovate in ways they had never imagined.

Explanation of Concepts

1. **Magical Kingdom with Spells**: Ethereum is like a magical kingdom where not only can you exchange coins, but you can also create and run automated spells (smart contracts) that perform various tasks automatically.
2. **Automated Spells and Tools**: Ethereum allows for the creation and execution of smart contracts and decentralized applications (dApps), which are automated tools that can perform a wide range of functions without needing a central authority.
3. **Self-Executing Agreement**: A smart contract is a self-executing agreement with the terms directly written into code. It automatically enforces the terms when predefined conditions are met, ensuring that agreements are honored without needing intermediaries.
4. **Decentralized Applications**: dApps are applications that run on the Ethereum network and can perform a wide range of functions. They offer enhanced security and transparency compared to traditional apps because they operate on a decentralized network.
5. **Incentive Coins**: The coins used in Ethereum are called Ether. They are used to pay for transactions, execute smart contracts, and incentivize participants who help maintain the network, ensuring that it runs smoothly and resources are allocated efficiently.
6. **Flexibility and Security**: Ethereum's flexibility allows developers to create innovative solutions, while its decentralized nature ensures that applications are secure

and free from censorship, providing a trustworthy platform for various digital applications.
7. **Token Creation**: Ethereum supports the creation of tokens, allowing anyone to create their own digital assets that can represent anything from currency to ownership rights, providing new opportunities for digital innovation and asset management.

Questions

1. What is Ethereum, and how is it different from regular cryptocurrency?

    A. It's just another type of digital coin like Bitcoin.

    B. It's a magical kingdom where you can not only exchange coins but also create and run automated spells called smart contracts.

    C. It's a platform only for gaming.

2. What are smart contracts, and how do they work on Ethereum?

    A. Contracts that must be signed with a pen and paper.

    B. Self-executing agreements with the terms directly written into code, automatically enforcing the terms when conditions are met.

    C. Contracts that can be changed by anyone at any time.

3. What are decentralized applications (dApps) in Ethereum?

    A. Regular apps that you download from the app store.

    B. Applications that run on the Ethereum network without needing a central authority, offering enhanced security and transparency.

C. Apps that require a central server to function.

4. What is Ether, and what is it used for in the Ethereum network?

   A. It's a type of physical currency used in the real world.

   B. The coins used in Ethereum to pay for transactions, execute smart contracts, and incentivize participants who help maintain the network.

   C. A magical potion used in video games.

5. How does Ethereum support innovation and security?

   A. By limiting what developers can create on the platform.

   B. By allowing developers to create a wide range of innovative solutions with its flexible platform, while its decentralized nature ensures security and freedom from censorship.

   C. By restricting access to only government-approved applications.

Answers

1. **B** - Ethereum is a magical kingdom where you can not only exchange coins but also create and run automated spells called smart contracts.
2. **B** - Smart contracts are self-executing agreements with the terms directly written into code, automatically enforcing the terms when conditions are met.
3. **B** - Decentralized applications (dApps) run on the Ethereum network without needing a central authority, offering enhanced security and transparency.
4. **B** - Ether is the coin used in Ethereum to pay for transactions, execute smart contracts, and incentivize participants who help maintain the network.
5. **B** - Ethereum supports innovation by allowing developers to create a wide range of solutions, and its decentralized nature ensures that applications are secure and free from censorship.

Alternatives and Variety

A rainbow appeared over the forest, its vibrant colors dancing in the sky, catching the eye of Robbie Rabbit as he hopped along with his feathered hat bouncing on his head. He clutched a scroll tightly, clearly excited to share its contents. He hurried over to Barry Bear and Kylie Kangaroo, who were playing a game of tag.

"Barry! Kylie! The Wise Old Wizard has sent us on another quest!" Robbie exclaimed, his excitement barely contained.

Kylie tilted her head. "What's it about this time, Robbie?"

"It's about something called Altcoins! We need to learn what they are and how they work!" Robbie said, his eyes twinkling with curiosity.

"Altcoins? That sounds fascinating," Barry replied, setting aside his game.

They made their way to the Wise Old Wizard's tower, where the Wizard greeted them warmly, his eyes sparkling with wisdom.

"Ah, Barry, Robbie, and Kylie, welcome," the Wizard began. "Today, we will explore the concept of Altcoins and understand their significance."

Kylie hopped in place. "What are Altcoins, and how do they work?"

The Wizard nodded. "Imagine a magical land where, in addition to the well-known gold coins, there are various other types of enchanted coins, each with its own unique properties and uses. These are called Altcoins (alternative enchanted coins)."

Robbie's ears perked up. "So, they're like special coins with different powers?"

"Exactly, Robbie," the Wizard replied. "Let's start with the basics. Altcoins are alternative digital currencies to the most famous one, which is often compared to gold. Each Altcoin operates on its own unique system and has specific features that set it apart (alternative digital currencies)."

With a wave of the Wizard's staff, a shimmering portal opened, leading them into a grand hall filled with creatures trading and using various types of enchanted coins.

"First, let's explore some well-known Altcoins," the Wizard said, leading them to a group of foxes and rabbits discussing different coins. "There are many types of Altcoins, such as those focused on privacy, faster transactions, or unique applications. Each serves a different purpose in the magical land (diverse purposes)."

Barry watched as the foxes and rabbits compared different Altcoins. "So, each coin has its own special use?"

"Precisely, Barry," the Wizard replied. "Next, let's talk about how these coins are created and maintained. Like the original digital gold coin, Altcoins are created through a process that involves solving complex puzzles to add new blocks to a chain, and they operate on their own decentralized networks (creation and maintenance)."

They moved to another section of the hall where a group of squirrels were solving puzzles and maintaining the Altcoin chains. "This ensures that the Altcoins are secure and that transactions are verified and recorded accurately (security and verification)," the Wizard explained.

Robbie hopped around the hall. "What makes people use these different coins?"

The Wizard smiled. "Altcoins offer various benefits, such as improved transaction speeds, enhanced privacy, or specialized uses for different applications. They provide options for different needs and preferences in the magical land (benefits and options)."

They arrived at a station where a rabbit was demonstrating the use of an Altcoin for a specific application. "Some Altcoins are designed for particular uses, like buying enchanted items or accessing certain services, making them valuable in different ways (specialized uses)," the Wizard explained.

Barry saw the rabbit show how transactions with Altcoins were quick and efficient. "So, Altcoins are like different tools for different jobs?"

"Exactly," the Wizard replied. "Now, let's talk about the flexibility of Altcoins. Their unique features and applications make them adaptable to various needs, from everyday transactions to specialized tasks in the magical land (flexibility and adaptability)."

Robbie clapped his paws. "This is amazing! What else?"

The Wizard nodded. "Let's discuss the future potential of Altcoins. As new coins are created and their uses evolve, they offer innovative solutions and possibilities for the creatures of the magical land (future potential)."

Barry and Robbie spent the rest of the day exploring the world of Altcoins, amazed by their structure, operation, and impact. Even Kylie began to show interest, asking questions and engaging with the demonstrations. By the time the sun began to set, they felt enlightened and excited about the possibilities.

As they made their way back through the portal, Robbie couldn't help but make Barry and Kylie laugh with his impressions of the Wise Old Wizard explaining Altcoins.

Barry, feeling wiser and more informed, knew that with the knowledge of these technologies, they could explore and innovate in ways they had never imagined.

Explanation of Concepts

1. **Alternative Enchanted Coins**: Altcoins are alternative digital currencies to the most famous one, which is often compared to gold. Each Altcoin operates on its own unique system and has specific features that set it apart.
2. **Diverse Purposes**: There are many types of Altcoins, each serving a different purpose in the digital world. Some focus on privacy, faster transactions, or unique applications, providing various uses and benefits.
3. **Creation and Maintenance**: Like the original digital gold coin, Altcoins are created through a process that involves solving complex puzzles to add new blocks to a chain. They operate on their own decentralized networks, ensuring security and verification.
4. **Security and Verification**: The process of creating and maintaining Altcoins ensures that they are secure and that transactions are verified and recorded accurately. This decentralized approach enhances trust and reliability.
5. **Benefits and Options**: Altcoins offer various benefits, such as improved transaction speeds, enhanced privacy, or specialized uses for different applications. They provide options for different needs and preferences in the digital world.
6. **Specialized Uses**: Some Altcoins are designed for particular uses, like buying specific items or accessing certain services, making them valuable in different ways. This specialization enhances their utility and appeal.

7. **Flexibility and Adaptability**: The unique features and applications of Altcoins make them adaptable to various needs, from everyday transactions to specialized tasks. This flexibility allows for innovative solutions and broader applications.
8. **Future Potential**: As new Altcoins are created and their uses evolve, they offer innovative solutions and possibilities for the digital world. Their future potential lies in their ability to address emerging needs and challenges.

Questions

1. What are Altcoins, and how do they differ from the original digital gold coin?

    A. They are just another name for the original digital gold coin.

    B. Altcoins are alternative digital currencies with unique systems and features that set them apart from the original digital gold coin.

    C. Altcoins are physical coins used in the real world.

2. What are some of the diverse purposes that Altcoins serve?

    A. Altcoins are only used for buying groceries.

    B. Some Altcoins focus on privacy, faster transactions, or unique applications, each serving a different purpose in the digital world.

    C. Altcoins are only used for playing games.

3. How are Altcoins created and maintained?

    A. They are created by printing money at a bank.

    B. Altcoins are created through a process that involves solving complex puzzles to add new blocks to a chain, operating on their own decentralized networks.

C. Altcoins are created by drawing them on paper.

4. What are some of the benefits and options that Altcoins provide?

    A. They have no benefits and are rarely used.

    B. Altcoins offer various benefits such as improved transaction speeds, enhanced privacy, or specialized uses for different applications, providing options for different needs.

    C. Altcoins are only used for decoration.

5. What potential do Altcoins have for the future?

    A. Altcoins have no future and will disappear soon.

    B. Altcoins offer innovative solutions and possibilities for the digital world as new coins are created and their uses evolve, addressing emerging needs and challenges.

    C. Altcoins are only used in the past and have no relevance today.

Answers

1. **B** - Altcoins are alternative digital currencies with unique systems and features that set them apart from the original digital gold coin.

2. **B** - Some Altcoins focus on privacy, faster transactions, or unique applications, each serving a different purpose in the digital world.
3. **B** - Altcoins are created through a process that involves solving complex puzzles to add new blocks to a chain, operating on their own decentralized networks.
4. **B** - Altcoins offer various benefits such as improved transaction speeds, enhanced privacy, or specialized uses for different applications, providing options for different needs.
5. **B** - Altcoins offer innovative solutions and possibilities for the digital world as new coins are created and their uses evolve, addressing emerging needs and challenges.

Tokens Transform Friends

A sudden burst of laughter echoed through the forest as a group of squirrels tumbled down from the branches, chasing each other playfully. Robbie Rabbit, his feathered hat perched jauntily on his head, emerged from the bushes holding a scroll with great excitement. He hurried over to Barry Bear and Kylie Kangaroo, who were having a friendly race.

"Barry! Kylie! The Wise Old Wizard has sent us on another quest!" Robbie exclaimed, practically bouncing with anticipation.

Kylie tilted her head. "What's it about this time, Robbie?"

"It's about something called Tokens! We need to learn what they are and how they work!" Robbie said, his eyes shining with curiosity.

"Tokens? That sounds fascinating," Barry replied, setting aside their race.

They made their way to the Wise Old Wizard's tower, where the Wizard greeted them warmly, his eyes twinkling with wisdom.

"Ah, Barry, Robbie, and Kylie, welcome," the Wizard began. "Today, we will explore the concept of Tokens and understand their significance."

Kylie hopped in place. "What are Tokens, and how do they work?"

The Wizard nodded. "Imagine a magical kingdom where, in addition to regular coins, there are special tokens that grant you access to different experiences, services, or even voting rights in the kingdom's decisions. These are called Tokens (special tokens)."

Robbie's ears perked up. "So, they're like magical tickets?"

"Exactly, Robbie," the Wizard replied. "Let's start with the basics. A token is a digital representation of value, utility, or an asset that is created and managed on a blockchain. They can represent anything from currency, access rights, to ownership of assets (digital representation)."

With a wave of the Wizard's staff, a shimmering portal opened, leading them into a grand hall filled with creatures using various types of tokens for different activities.

"First, let's explore utility tokens," the Wizard said, leading them to a group of foxes and rabbits using tokens to access enchanted games and services. "Utility tokens grant access to specific services or products within a platform. They are like magical tickets that let you use different enchanted tools and experiences (utility tokens)."

Barry watched as the foxes and rabbits played games and used various services with their tokens. "So, utility tokens are used for accessing different things?"

"Precisely, Barry," the Wizard replied. "Next, let's talk about security tokens. These represent ownership in an asset, such as a piece of land or a share in a treasure. They are like deeds or certificates that show you own something valuable (security tokens)."

They moved to another section of the hall where a group of squirrels were managing their ownership rights using tokens. "Security tokens ensure that ownership is secure and can be easily transferred or sold," the Wizard explained.

Robbie hopped around the hall. "What about tokens that can be used for voting or decision-making?"

The Wizard smiled. "Those are governance tokens. They allow the holders to participate in the decision-making processes of a community or project. It's like having a say in how the magical kingdom is run (governance tokens)."

They arrived at a station where a rabbit was demonstrating how governance tokens were used to vote on new projects and rules. "Governance tokens ensure that the community has a voice in important decisions," the Wizard explained.

Barry saw the rabbit show how voting was quick and fair. "So, governance tokens are like votes in the kingdom?"

"Exactly," the Wizard replied. "Now, let's talk about the benefits of tokens. They provide flexibility and security, enabling various applications such as fundraising, access control, and more. Tokens can be customized to fit different needs and purposes (flexibility and security)."

Robbie clapped his paws. "This is amazing! What else?"

The Wizard nodded. "Tokens also enable the creation of decentralized applications and ecosystems where participants can interact and transact without needing intermediaries. This enhances efficiency and trust within the magical land (decentralized applications)."

Barry and Robbie spent the rest of the day exploring the world of tokens, amazed by their structure, operation, and impact. Even Kylie began to show interest, asking questions and engaging with the demonstrations. By the time the sun began to set, they felt enlightened and excited about the possibilities.

As they made their way back through the portal, Robbie couldn't help but make Barry and Kylie laugh with his impressions of the Wise Old Wizard explaining tokens.

Barry, feeling wiser and more informed, knew that with the knowledge of these technologies, they could explore and innovate in ways they had never imagined.

Explanation of Concepts

1. **Special Tokens**: Tokens are like special magical tickets that grant access to different experiences, services, or even voting rights. They are digital representations of value, utility, or assets created and managed on a blockchain.
2. **Digital Representation**: A token is a digital representation of value, utility, or an asset. Tokens can represent anything from currency and access rights to ownership of assets, and they are created and managed on a blockchain.
3. **Utility Tokens**: Utility tokens grant access to specific services or products within a platform. They act like magical tickets that let users access different enchanted tools and experiences.
4. **Security Tokens**: Security tokens represent ownership in an asset, such as a piece of land or a share in a treasure. They function like deeds or certificates that indicate ownership of something valuable.
5. **Governance Tokens**: Governance tokens allow holders to participate in decision-making processes of a community or project. They are like votes that give the community a voice in important decisions.
6. **Flexibility and Security**: Tokens provide flexibility and security, enabling various applications such as fundraising, access control, and more. They can be customized to fit different needs and purposes.
7. **Decentralized Applications**: Tokens enable the creation of decentralized applications and ecosystems

where participants can interact and transact without intermediaries, enhancing efficiency and trust.

Questions

1. What are tokens in the magical kingdom, and what do they represent?

    A. Tokens are regular coins used for buying things.

    B. Tokens are digital representations of value, utility, or assets, created and managed on a blockchain.

    C. Tokens are only used for playing games.

2. What is the purpose of utility tokens in the magical kingdom?

    A. Utility tokens are used for decoration.

    B. Utility tokens grant access to specific services or products within a platform, like magical tickets.

    C. Utility tokens are only used to store information.

3. How do security tokens function in the magical kingdom?

    A. Security tokens represent ownership in an asset, such as a piece of land or a share in a treasure, functioning like deeds or certificates.

    B. Security tokens are used for trading games.

    C. Security tokens have no value.

4. What role do governance tokens play in the decision-making process?

A. Governance tokens are used for voting in the kingdom, allowing holders to participate in important decisions.

B. Governance tokens are used for playing with friends.

C. Governance tokens have no special function.

5. How do tokens contribute to the creation of decentralized applications?

A. Tokens are used to create maps.

B. Tokens enable the creation of decentralized applications where participants can interact and transact without intermediaries, enhancing efficiency and trust.

C. Tokens have no role in decentralized applications.

Answers

1. **B** - Tokens are digital representations of value, utility, or assets, created and managed on a blockchain.
2. **B** - Utility tokens grant access to specific services or products within a platform, like magical tickets.
3. **A** - Security tokens represent ownership in an asset, such as a piece of land or a share in a treasure, functioning like deeds or certificates.

4. **A** - Governance tokens are used for voting in the kingdom, allowing holders to participate in important decisions.
5. **B** - Tokens enable the creation of decentralized applications where participants can interact and transact without intermediaries, enhancing efficiency and trust.

Purses, Keys, and Wallets

A sudden whoosh of wind sent leaves swirling through the air, making Robbie Rabbit's feathered hat dance atop his head. He emerged from the bushes, clutching a scroll with great excitement. He hurried over to Barry Bear and Kylie Kangaroo, who were playing a game of hopscotch.

"Barry! Kylie! The Wise Old Wizard has sent us on another quest!" Robbie exclaimed, practically bouncing with anticipation.

Kylie tilted her head. "What's it about this time, Robbie?"

"It's about something called a Wallet! We need to learn what it is and how it works!" Robbie said, his eyes twinkling with curiosity.

"A Wallet? That sounds fascinating," Barry replied, setting aside their game.

They made their way to the Wise Old Wizard's tower, where the Wizard greeted them warmly, his eyes sparkling with wisdom.

"Ah, Barry, Robbie, and Kylie, welcome," the Wizard began. "Today, we will explore the concept of a Wallet and understand its significance."

Kylie hopped in place. "What is a Wallet, and how does it work?"

The Wizard nodded. "Imagine a magical pouch that can store not just gold coins but also enchanted keys that unlock different treasures and secrets. This is similar to what a Wallet does in the digital realm (magical pouch)."

Robbie's ears perked up. "So, it's like a special bag for keeping things safe?"

"Exactly, Robbie," the Wizard replied. "Let's start with the basics. A Wallet is a digital tool that stores your unique keys, allowing you to access and manage your digital coins and other assets (digital tool)."

With a wave of the Wizard's staff, a shimmering portal opened, leading them into a grand hall filled with creatures managing their magical pouches.

"First, let's explore how Wallets work," the Wizard said, leading them to a group of foxes and rabbits using their pouches to access various treasures. "A Wallet contains two types of keys: a public key, which is like your address, and a private key, which is like your secret password (public key, private key)."

Barry watched as the foxes and rabbits accessed their treasures effortlessly. "So, the public key is like an address, and the private key is a secret password?"

"Precisely, Barry," the Wizard replied. "Next, let's talk about how transactions are made. When you want to send or receive digital coins, you use your private key to authorize the transaction, ensuring that only you can access your assets (transaction authorization)."

They moved to another section of the hall where a group of squirrels were demonstrating transactions with their pouches. "This process ensures that your digital coins are secure and can only be accessed by you," the Wizard explained.

Robbie hopped around the hall. "What about keeping the keys safe? What happens if you lose them?"

The Wizard smiled. "That's an important question, Robbie. Keeping your private key safe is crucial because if you lose it, you lose access to your digital coins. This is why many use special storage methods, like hardware wallets or secure software, to protect their keys (key protection)."

They arrived at a station where a rabbit was demonstrating different ways to keep keys safe. "Some use hardware wallets, which are physical devices, while others use secure software wallets," the Wizard explained.

Barry saw the rabbit show how to store keys in different ways. "So, it's important to keep the keys safe to protect your assets?"

"Exactly," the Wizard replied. "Now, let's talk about the benefits of using a Wallet. It allows you to manage and control your digital coins securely and conveniently. You can send and receive coins easily, track your balance, and keep your assets safe (asset management)."

Robbie clapped his paws. "This is amazing! What else?"

The Wizard nodded. "Wallets also enable participation in decentralized applications and ecosystems, where you can interact and transact without intermediaries. This enhances efficiency and trust in the magical land (decentralized applications)."

Barry and Robbie spent the rest of the day exploring the world of Wallets, amazed by their structure, operation, and impact. Even Kylie began to show interest, asking questions and engaging with the demonstrations. By the time the sun began to set, they felt enlightened and excited about the possibilities.

As they made their way back through the portal, Robbie couldn't help but make Barry and Kylie laugh with his impressions of the Wise Old Wizard explaining Wallets.

Barry, feeling wiser and more informed, knew that with the knowledge of these technologies, they could explore and innovate in ways they had never imagined.

Explanation of Concepts

1. **Magical Pouch**: A Wallet is like a magical pouch that stores your unique keys, allowing you to access and manage your digital coins and other assets. It provides a secure way to store and use your digital wealth.
2. **Digital Tool**: A Wallet is a digital tool that stores your unique keys. It includes a public key, which acts like an address, and a private key, which is like a secret password. These keys enable secure access and management of digital assets.
3. **Public Key, Private Key**: The public key is like your address that you share with others to receive digital coins, while the private key is a secret password that you use to authorize transactions and access your assets.
4. **Transaction Authorization**: When you want to send or receive digital coins, you use your private key to authorize the transaction. This ensures that only you can access and control your digital assets, keeping them secure.
5. **Key Protection**: Keeping your private key safe is crucial because losing it means losing access to your digital coins. Special storage methods, like hardware wallets (physical devices) or secure software wallets, help protect your keys.
6. **Asset Management**: A Wallet allows you to manage and control your digital coins securely and conveniently. You can send and receive coins, track your balance, and keep your assets safe, making it a powerful tool for managing digital wealth.

7. **Decentralized Applications**: Wallets enable participation in decentralized applications and ecosystems, where you can interact and transact without intermediaries. This enhances efficiency and trust, providing more freedom in the digital realm.

Questions

1. What is a Wallet in the magical land, and what does it store?

    A. A Wallet is a physical pouch that stores coins.

    B. A Wallet is a digital tool that stores unique keys, allowing you to access and manage digital coins and assets.

    C. A Wallet is a book that contains spells.

2. What are the two types of keys stored in a Wallet, and what are their purposes?

    A. A silver key for unlocking doors and a golden key for accessing treasures.

    B. A public key, which acts like an address for receiving coins, and a private key, which is a secret password for authorizing transactions.

    C. A magic key for summoning creatures and a secret key for hiding.

3. Why is it important to keep your private key safe in the digital realm?

    A. Because losing it will unlock hidden treasures.

    B. Because losing it means you lose access to your digital coins and assets.

C. Because it allows you to fly.

4. How does a Wallet help in managing digital coins?

A. It organizes spells and potions.

B. It allows you to send and receive coins, track your balance, and keep your assets safe.

C. It turns coins into gold.

5. What role does a Wallet play in decentralized applications?

A. It creates new games to play.

B. It enables participation in decentralized applications, allowing you to interact and transact without intermediaries.

C. It decorates your digital house.

Answers

1. **B** - A Wallet is a digital tool that stores unique keys, allowing you to access and manage digital coins and assets.
2. **B** - A public key acts like an address for receiving coins, and a private key is a secret password for authorizing transactions.
3. **B** - It is important to keep your private key safe because losing it means you lose access to your digital coins and assets.
4. **B** - A Wallet helps in managing digital coins by allowing you to send and receive coins, track your balance, and keep your assets safe.
5. **B** - A Wallet enables participation in decentralized applications, allowing you to interact and transact without intermediaries.

Keys Open Doors

The sun had just begun its descent, casting a golden hue over the forest. Robbie Rabbit, with his feathered hat perched jauntily on his head, emerged from the bushes holding a scroll with great excitement. He hurried over to Barry Bear and Kylie Kangaroo, who were playing a game of hopscotch.

"Barry! Kylie! The Wise Old Wizard has sent us on another quest!" Robbie exclaimed, practically bouncing with anticipation.

Kylie tilted her head. "What's it about this time, Robbie?"

"It's about something called a Private Key! We need to learn what it is and how it works!" Robbie said, his eyes twinkling with curiosity.

"A Private Key? That sounds intriguing," Barry replied, setting aside their game.

They made their way to the Wise Old Wizard's tower, where the Wizard greeted them warmly, his eyes sparkling with wisdom.

"Ah, Barry, Robbie, and Kylie, welcome," the Wizard began. "Today, we will explore the concept of a Private Key and understand its significance."

Kylie hopped in place. "What is a Private Key, and how does it work?"

The Wizard nodded. "Imagine a magical kingdom where every treasure chest has a unique, invisible key that only the owner possesses. This key allows them to access their treasures and protect them from others. This is similar to what a Private Key does in the digital realm (invisible key)."

Robbie's ears perked up. "So, it's like a secret key for your treasures?"

"Exactly, Robbie," the Wizard replied. "Let's start with the basics. A Private Key is a secret code that allows you to access and manage your digital assets, like coins or tokens. It is crucial for ensuring the security of your digital wealth (secret code)."

With a wave of the Wizard's staff, a shimmering portal opened, leading them into a grand hall filled with creatures managing their enchanted chests.

"First, let's explore how Private Keys work," the Wizard said, leading them to a group of foxes and rabbits using their keys to open and secure their chests. "A Private Key is used to sign transactions, proving that you are the rightful owner of the assets and authorizing their movement (transaction signing)."

Barry watched as the foxes and rabbits accessed their treasures effortlessly. "So, the Private Key proves ownership and allows access?"

"Precisely, Barry," the Wizard replied. "Next, let's talk about the importance of keeping the Private Key safe. If someone else gets hold of your Private Key, they can access and steal your assets. This is why it's crucial to store it securely (security importance)."

They moved to another section of the hall where a group of squirrels were demonstrating different ways to keep their keys safe. "Some use physical devices like enchanted lockboxes, while others use secure spells to protect their keys (storage methods)," the Wizard explained.

Robbie hopped around the hall. "What if someone loses their Private Key?"

The Wizard frowned. "Losing a Private Key is like losing access to your treasure forever. There's no way to recover the assets without the key, which is why it's vital to keep backups in secure locations (irrevocable loss)."

They arrived at a station where a rabbit was demonstrating how to create and store backups of their keys. "Having a backup ensures that even if you lose one key, you can still access your assets with another (backup creation)," the Wizard explained.

Barry saw the rabbit show how to store keys in different ways. "So, it's important to keep the keys safe and have backups?"

"Exactly," the Wizard replied. "Now, let's talk about how Private Keys work with Public Keys. While the Private Key is kept secret, the Public Key can be shared with others to receive assets. The Public Key is derived from the Private

Key, ensuring they are uniquely linked (public-private relationship)."

Robbie clapped his paws. "This is amazing! What else?"

The Wizard nodded. "Private Keys enable secure transactions and ownership verification without needing a central authority, enhancing trust and security in the digital world (decentralized security)."

Barry and Robbie spent the rest of the day exploring the world of Private Keys, amazed by their structure, operation, and impact. Even Kylie began to show interest, asking questions and engaging with the demonstrations. By the time the sun began to set, they felt enlightened and excited about the possibilities.

As they made their way back through the portal, Robbie couldn't help but make Barry and Kylie laugh with his impressions of the Wise Old Wizard explaining Private Keys.

Barry, feeling wiser and more informed, knew that with the knowledge of these technologies, they could explore and innovate in ways they had never imagined.

Explanation of Concepts

1. **Invisible Key**: A Private Key is like an invisible key that only the owner possesses. It allows them to access and manage their digital assets, ensuring their security and privacy.
2. **Secret Code**: A Private Key is a secret code that enables access to digital assets like coins or tokens. It ensures the owner can securely manage and transfer their wealth.
3. **Transaction Signing**: A Private Key is used to sign transactions, proving ownership and authorizing the movement of digital assets. This ensures that only the rightful owner can access and use their assets.
4. **Security Importance**: Keeping the Private Key safe is crucial because if someone else gets hold of it, they can access and steal your assets. Secure storage methods are vital for protecting your key.
5. **Storage Methods**: Private Keys can be stored using physical devices like hardware wallets or secure software methods. These storage solutions help protect the key from unauthorized access and theft.
6. **Irrevocable Loss**: Losing a Private Key is like losing access to your treasure forever. There is no way to recover the assets without the key, highlighting the importance of secure backups.
7. **Backup Creation**: Creating and storing backups of Private Keys ensures that even if the original key is lost, the assets can still be accessed using the backup. This provides an extra layer of security.

8. **Public-Private Relationship**: The Public Key is derived from the Private Key and can be shared with others to receive assets. This relationship ensures secure transactions and ownership verification.
9. **Decentralized Security**: Private Keys enable secure transactions and ownership verification without needing a central authority. This decentralized approach enhances trust and security in the digital world.

Questions

1. What is a Private Key compared to in the magical kingdom?

    A. A key that opens all doors.

    B. An invisible key that allows the owner to access and protect their treasures.

    C. A key that can be shared with anyone.

2. What is the main function of a Private Key in the digital realm?

    A. To create new coins.

    B. To sign transactions and prove ownership of digital assets.

    C. To unlock doors in the real world.

3. Why is it important to keep the Private Key safe?

    A. Because it will disappear if not used frequently.

    B. Because losing it means losing access to digital assets forever.

    C. Because it can be replaced easily.

4. What happens if someone else gains access to your Private Key?

    A. They can view your digital assets but cannot use them.

B. They can steal or use your digital assets.

C. They can change your Public Key.

5. How are the Private Key and Public Key related?

   A. The Public Key is randomly created and unrelated to the Private Key.

   B. The Public Key is derived from the Private Key and can be shared with others to receive assets.

   C. The Private Key comes from the Public Key and is shared with everyone.

Answers

1. **B** - A Private Key is compared to an invisible key that allows the owner to access and protect their treasures.
2. **B** - The main function of a Private Key is to sign transactions and prove ownership of digital assets.
3. **B** - It is important to keep the Private Key safe because losing it means losing access to digital assets forever.
4. **B** - If someone else gains access to your Private Key, they can steal or use your digital assets.
5. **B** - The Public Key is derived from the Private Key and can be shared with others to receive assets.

Public Service Addresses

A sudden burst of laughter filled the air as a group of squirrels chased each other through the trees. Robbie Rabbit, with his feathered hat bouncing on his head, emerged from the bushes holding a scroll with great excitement. He hurried over to Barry Bear, Kylie Kangaroo, and a playful panda named Pippa, who were playing a game of tag.

"Barry! Kylie! Pippa! The Wise Old Wizard has sent us on another quest!" Robbie exclaimed, practically bouncing with anticipation.

Pippa rolled onto her back, laughing. "What's it about this time, Robbie?"

"It's about something called a Public Key! We need to learn what it is and how it works!" Robbie said, his eyes twinkling with curiosity.

"A Public Key? That sounds fascinating," Barry replied, setting aside their game.

They made their way to the Wise Old Wizard's tower, where the Wizard greeted them warmly, his eyes sparkling with wisdom.

"Ah, Barry, Robbie, Kylie, and Pippa, welcome," the Wizard began. "Today, we will explore the concept of a Public Key and understand its significance."

Kylie hopped in place. "What is a Public Key, and how does it work?"

The Wizard nodded. "Imagine a magical land where everyone has a unique address that they can share with others to receive letters, gifts, or messages. This is similar to what a Public Key does in the digital realm (unique address)."

Robbie's ears perked up. "So, it's like a special address for receiving treasures?"

"Exactly, Robbie," the Wizard replied. "Let's start with the basics. A Public Key is a digital address that you can share with others so they can send you digital assets, like coins or tokens (digital address)."

With a wave of the Wizard's staff, a shimmering portal opened, leading them into a grand hall filled with creatures sending and receiving enchanted parcels.

"First, let's explore how Public Keys work," the Wizard said, leading them to a group of foxes and rabbits using their addresses to send and receive magical items. "A Public Key is derived from a Private Key, ensuring they are uniquely linked. The Public Key is shared openly, while the Private Key remains secret to ensure security (linked keys)."

Barry watched as the foxes and rabbits received their parcels effortlessly. "So, the Public Key is shared, and the Private Key stays secret?"

"Precisely, Barry," the Wizard replied. "Next, let's talk about the importance of Public Keys in transactions. When someone wants to send you digital assets, they use your Public Key to direct the assets to your address (transaction direction)."

They moved to another section of the hall where a group of squirrels were demonstrating transactions with their addresses. "This process ensures that only you can receive the assets sent to your Public Key, while the Private Key allows you to access and manage them (security and access)," the Wizard explained.

Robbie hopped around the hall. "What if someone tries to send assets to the wrong address?"

The Wizard smiled. "That's why it's important to share your correct Public Key. Each Public Key is unique, and sending assets to the wrong address means they might end up in the wrong hands or be lost forever (address accuracy)."

They arrived at a station where a rabbit was demonstrating how to share their Public Key safely. "Sharing your Public Key allows others to send you assets without compromising your security, as the Private Key remains secret (safe sharing)," the Wizard explained.

Pippa saw the rabbit show how to share addresses in different ways. "So, it's important to share the correct address to ensure the assets reach you?"

"Exactly," the Wizard replied. "Now, let's talk about the benefits of using Public Keys. They enable secure, transparent, and efficient transactions without needing a central authority. This enhances trust and security in the digital world (secure transactions)."

Robbie clapped his paws. "This is amazing! What else?"

The Wizard nodded. "Public Keys also support the development of decentralized applications and ecosystems, where participants can interact and transact directly with each other. This fosters innovation and efficiency (decentralized applications)."

Barry and Robbie spent the rest of the day exploring the world of Public Keys, amazed by their structure, operation, and impact. Even Kylie and Pippa began to show interest, asking questions and engaging with the demonstrations. By the time the sun began to set, they felt enlightened and excited about the possibilities.

As they made their way back through the portal, Robbie couldn't help but make Barry, Kylie, and Pippa laugh with his impressions of the Wise Old Wizard explaining Public Keys.

Barry, feeling wiser and more informed, knew that with the knowledge of these technologies, they could explore and innovate in ways they had never imagined.

Explanation of Concepts

1. **Unique Address**: A Public Key is like a unique address that you can share with others to receive digital assets, such as coins or tokens. It is a digital identifier that facilitates secure transactions.
2. **Digital Address**: A Public Key is a digital address derived from a Private Key, ensuring they are uniquely linked. The Public Key is shared openly to receive assets, while the Private Key remains secret to ensure security.
3. **Linked Keys**: The Public Key and Private Key are linked, with the Public Key being shared openly and the Private Key kept secret. This linkage ensures secure and verifiable transactions.
4. **Transaction Direction**: When someone wants to send you digital assets, they use your Public Key to direct the assets to your address. This process ensures that only the intended recipient can receive the assets.
5. **Security and Access**: The Public Key allows others to send you assets, while the Private Key allows you to access and manage them. This separation ensures security and control over your digital assets.
6. **Address Accuracy**: Sharing the correct Public Key is crucial to ensure that assets reach the intended recipient. Sending assets to the wrong address can result in loss or misdirection.
7. **Safe Sharing**: Sharing your Public Key allows others to send you assets without compromising your security, as the Private Key remains secret. This enables safe and secure transactions.

8. **Secure Transactions**: Public Keys enable secure, transparent, and efficient transactions without needing a central authority. This enhances trust and security in the digital world.
9. **Decentralized Applications**: Public Keys support the development of decentralized applications and ecosystems, where participants can interact and transact directly with each other, fostering innovation and efficiency.

Questions

1. What is a Public Key most similar to in the story?

    A. A secret code shared with everyone

    B. A unique address for receiving digital assets

    C. A treasure map that leads to hidden coins

2. How are the Public Key and Private Key linked?

    A. They are the same key used for sending and receiving assets

    B. The Public Key is shared openly, and the Private Key is kept secret

    C. The Private Key can be shared with anyone, but the Public Key must remain secret

3. What happens if someone sends assets to the wrong Public Key?

    A. The assets can be retrieved easily by contacting the sender

    B. The assets may be lost or sent to the wrong person

    C. The system automatically corrects the mistake

4. Why is it important to share your Public Key safely?

    A. To ensure only friends know your secret code

B. So others can send you assets without compromising your Private Key

C. To prevent losing your Public Key forever

5. What is one benefit of using Public Keys for transactions?

A. They make transactions completely anonymous with no trace

B. They enable secure, transparent transactions without needing a central authority

C. They allow anyone to access your Private Key and manage your assets

Answers

1. **B** - A unique address for receiving digital assets
2. **B** - The Public Key is shared openly, and the Private Key is kept secret
3. **B** - The assets may be lost or sent to the wrong person
4. **B** - So others can send you assets without compromising your Private Key
5. **B** - They enable secure, transparent transactions without needing a central authority

Enchanted Address Quest

The sound of a babbling brook filled the air as Robbie Rabbit, with his feathered hat bobbing cheerfully, emerged from behind a large oak tree holding a scroll. He hurried over to Barry Bear, Kylie Kangaroo, and Pippa the playful panda, who were busy building a makeshift bridge across the brook.

"Barry! Kylie! Pippa! The Wise Old Wizard has sent us on another quest!" Robbie exclaimed, practically hopping in excitement.

Pippa tumbled over, her paws clapping. "What's it about this time, Robbie?"

"It's about something called an Address! We need to learn what it is and how it works!" Robbie said, his eyes gleaming with curiosity.

"An Address? That sounds interesting," Barry replied, setting down a large stick.

They made their way to the Wise Old Wizard's tower, where the Wizard greeted them warmly, his eyes twinkling with wisdom.

"Ah, Barry, Robbie, Kylie, and Pippa, welcome," the Wizard began. "Today, we will explore the concept of an Address and understand its significance."

Kylie hopped in place. "What is an Address, and how does it work?"

The Wizard nodded. "Imagine a magical land where everyone has a unique location that can be shared with others to receive letters, gifts, or messages. This unique location is similar to what an Address does in the digital realm (unique location)."

Robbie's ears perked up. "So, it's like a special place for receiving treasures?"

"Exactly, Robbie," the Wizard replied. "Let's start with the basics. An Address is a unique identifier that you can share with others so they can send you digital assets, like coins or tokens (unique identifier)."

With a wave of the Wizard's staff, a shimmering portal opened, leading them into a grand hall filled with creatures sending and receiving enchanted parcels.

"First, let's explore how Addresses work," the Wizard said, leading them to a group of foxes and rabbits using their addresses to send and receive magical items. "An Address is generated from a Private Key and Public Key, ensuring it is unique and secure. It acts as the destination for digital assets (generated address)."

Barry watched as the foxes and rabbits received their parcels effortlessly. "So, the Address is where the digital treasures are sent?"

"Precisely, Barry," the Wizard replied. "Next, let's talk about the importance of Addresses in transactions. When someone wants to send you digital assets, they use your Address to direct the assets to your location (transaction direction)."

They moved to another section of the hall where a group of squirrels were demonstrating transactions with their addresses. "This process ensures that only you can receive the assets sent to your Address, providing security and accuracy (security and accuracy)," the Wizard explained.

Robbie hopped around the hall. "What if someone sends assets to the wrong Address?"

The Wizard frowned slightly. "That's why it's important to share your correct Address. Each Address is unique, and sending assets to the wrong Address means they might end up in the wrong hands or be lost forever (address accuracy)."

They arrived at a station where a rabbit was demonstrating how to share their Address safely. "Sharing your Address allows others to send you assets without compromising your security, as only the correct Address can receive the assets (safe sharing)," the Wizard explained.

Pippa saw the rabbit show how to share addresses in different ways. "So, it's important to share the correct Address to ensure the assets reach you?"

"Exactly," the Wizard replied. "Now, let's talk about the benefits of using Addresses. They enable secure, transparent, and efficient transactions without needing a central authority. This enhances trust and security in the digital world (secure transactions)."

Robbie clapped his paws. "This is amazing! What else?"

The Wizard nodded. "Addresses also support the development of decentralized applications and ecosystems, where participants can interact and transact directly with each other. This fosters innovation and efficiency (decentralized applications)."

Barry and Robbie spent the rest of the day exploring the world of Addresses, amazed by their structure, operation, and impact. Even Kylie and Pippa began to show interest, asking questions and engaging with the demonstrations. By the time the sun began to set, they felt enlightened and excited about the possibilities.

As they made their way back through the portal, Robbie couldn't help but make Barry, Kylie, and Pippa laugh with his impressions of the Wise Old Wizard explaining Addresses.

Barry, feeling wiser and more informed, knew that with the knowledge of these technologies, they could explore and innovate in ways they had never imagined.

Explanation of Concepts

1. **Unique Location**: An Address in the digital realm is like a unique location where digital assets can be sent. It acts as a destination for receiving digital treasures.
2. **Unique Identifier**: An Address is a unique identifier that can be shared with others so they can send digital assets like coins or tokens. It ensures that each transaction is directed to the correct recipient.
3. **Generated Address**: An Address is generated from a Private Key and Public Key, ensuring it is unique and secure. This generation process links the Address to the owner's keys.
4. **Transaction Direction**: When someone wants to send digital assets, they use the recipient's Address to direct the assets. This ensures that the assets are sent to the correct destination.
5. **Security and Accuracy**: The Address provides security and accuracy in transactions. Only the correct Address can receive the assets, preventing loss or misdirection.
6. **Address Accuracy**: Sharing the correct Address is crucial to ensure that assets reach the intended recipient. Sending assets to the wrong Address can result in loss or misdirection.
7. **Safe Sharing**: Sharing your Address allows others to send you assets without compromising your security. The Address ensures that only the intended recipient can receive the assets.
8. **Secure Transactions**: Addresses enable secure, transparent, and efficient transactions without needing a

central authority. This enhances trust and security in the digital world.
9. **Decentralized Applications**: Addresses support the development of decentralized applications and ecosystems, where participants can interact and transact directly with each other, fostering innovation and efficiency.

Questions

1. What is a Public Key compared to in the magical kingdom?

    A. A special potion.

    B. A unique address for receiving digital assets.

    C. A secret spell.

2. What is the relationship between a Public Key and a Private Key?

    A. They are identical and interchangeable.

    B. The Public Key is shared openly, while the Private Key is kept secret for security.

    C. The Private Key is used to receive assets, and the Public Key is never shared.

3. Why is it important to share the correct Public Key?

    A. To make sure you can send assets to others.

    B. To ensure that assets reach the intended recipient and aren't lost or misdirected.

    C. To store more assets in one place.

4. How does a Public Key help with secure transactions?

    A. It automatically completes all transactions without user input.

B. It allows others to send assets to you, while the Private Key ensures only you can access and manage them.

C. It sends assets back if the wrong Public Key is used.

5. What role do Public Keys play in decentralized applications (dApps)?

A. They allow participants to interact and transact directly without needing a central authority.

B. They store all information for the application.

C. They are used to send information only, not assets.

Answers

1. **B** - A Public Key is compared to a unique address for receiving digital assets.
2. **B** - The Public Key is shared openly, while the Private Key is kept secret for security.
3. **B** - It is important to share the correct Public Key to ensure that assets reach the intended recipient and aren't lost or misdirected.
4. **B** - A Public Key allows others to send assets to you, while the Private Key ensures only you can access and manage them.
5. **A** - Public Keys allow participants to interact and transact directly in decentralized applications without needing a central authority.

An Equivalent Exchange

The sound of a babbling brook filled the air as the morning sun peeked through the canopy. Robbie Rabbit, with his feathered hat bobbing cheerfully, emerged from behind a large bush holding a scroll. He hurried over to Barry Bear, Kylie Kangaroo, and Pippa the playful panda, who were busy building a makeshift raft by the river.

Robbie waved the scroll excitedly. "Guess what! We have a new mission!"

Pippa tumbled over, her paws clapping. "What's it about this time, Robbie?"

"It's about something called a Transaction! We need to learn what it is and how it works!" Robbie said, his eyes gleaming with curiosity.

"A Transaction? That sounds intriguing," Barry replied, setting down a large stick.

They made their way to the Wise Old Wizard's tower, where the Wizard greeted them warmly, his eyes twinkling with wisdom.

"Ah, Barry, Robbie, Kylie, and Pippa, welcome," the Wizard began. "Today, we will explore the concept of a Transaction and understand its significance."

Kylie hopped in place. "What is a Transaction, and how does it work?"

The Wizard nodded. "Imagine a magical land where creatures exchange enchanted items with each other. Each exchange is recorded in a grand book to ensure everyone knows who owns what. This exchange process is similar to what a Transaction does in the digital realm (exchange process)."

Robbie's ears perked up. "So, it's like trading treasures and keeping track of them?"

"Exactly, Robbie," the Wizard replied. "Let's start with the basics. A Transaction is the process of transferring digital assets from one party to another, and it is recorded on a ledger to keep track of ownership (digital asset transfer)."

With a wave of the Wizard's staff, a shimmering portal opened, leading them into a grand hall filled with creatures exchanging enchanted items.

"First, let's explore how Transactions work," the Wizard said, leading them to a group of foxes and rabbits making trades. "A Transaction involves three key elements: the sender, the receiver, and the amount of the asset being transferred (transaction elements)."

Barry watched as the foxes and rabbits completed their trades. "So, each trade has a sender, a receiver, and an amount?"

"Precisely, Barry," the Wizard replied. "Next, let's talk about how Transactions are verified. In our magical land, there are guardians who ensure that each trade is valid and that the sender has enough assets to make the trade. This verification process is called validation (validation)."

They moved to another section of the hall where a group of squirrels were acting as guardians, checking the trades. "This process ensures that all Transactions are legitimate and that no one is trying to trade more than they have (legitimacy and verification)," the Wizard explained.

Robbie hopped around the hall. "What happens once a Transaction is verified?"

The Wizard smiled. "Once a Transaction is verified, it is recorded in the grand book, also known as the ledger. This ensures that everyone can see the updated ownership of assets, making the system transparent and secure (recording and transparency)."

They arrived at a station where a rabbit was demonstrating how Transactions were recorded in the ledger. "Recording Transactions in the ledger ensures that everyone knows the current state of asset ownership," the Wizard explained.

Pippa saw the rabbit show how the ledger worked. "So, recording keeps everything clear and secure?"

"Exactly," the Wizard replied. "Now, let's talk about the benefits of Transactions. They enable secure, transparent, and efficient exchanges without needing a central authority. This enhances trust and security in the digital world (secure exchanges)."

Robbie clapped his paws. "This is amazing! What else?"

The Wizard nodded. "Transactions also support the development of decentralized applications and ecosystems, where participants can interact and transact directly with each other. This fosters innovation and efficiency (decentralized applications)."

Barry and Robbie spent the rest of the day exploring the world of Transactions, amazed by their structure, operation, and impact. Even Kylie and Pippa began to show interest, asking questions and engaging with the demonstrations. By the time the sun began to set, they felt enlightened and excited about the possibilities.

As they made their way back through the portal, Robbie couldn't help but make Barry, Kylie, and Pippa laugh with his impressions of the Wise Old Wizard explaining Transactions.

Barry, feeling wiser and more informed, knew that with the knowledge of these technologies, they could explore and innovate in ways they had never imagined.

Explanation of Concepts

1. **Exchange Process**: A Transaction is like trading treasures and keeping track of them in a magical book. It ensures that the exchange of digital assets is recorded and tracked accurately.
2. **Digital Asset Transfer**: A Transaction is the process of transferring digital assets from one party to another. It involves recording the transfer on a ledger to keep track of ownership and ensure transparency.
3. **Transaction Elements**: Each Transaction involves three key elements: the sender (who initiates the transfer), the receiver (who receives the assets), and the amount of the asset being transferred. These elements are essential for a valid transaction.
4. **Validation**: The validation process ensures that each Transaction is legitimate. Guardians (or validators) check that the sender has enough assets to make the trade and that the transaction is not fraudulent. This process maintains the integrity of the system.
5. **Legitimacy and Verification**: Verifying Transactions ensures that all trades are valid and no one is trying to transfer more assets than they have. This verification process prevents fraud and maintains trust in the system.
6. **Recording and Transparency**: Once a Transaction is verified, it is recorded in a ledger (or grand book). This recording keeps the system transparent and secure, allowing everyone to see the updated ownership of assets.

7. **Secure Exchanges**: Transactions enable secure, transparent, and efficient exchanges of digital assets without needing a central authority. This decentralized approach enhances trust and security in the digital world.
8. **Decentralized Applications**: Transactions support the development of decentralized applications and ecosystems, where participants can interact and transact directly with each other. This fosters innovation and efficiency, creating new opportunities for digital interaction.

Questions

1. What is a Transaction compared to in the magical land?

    A. Casting a spell

    B. Trading treasures and keeping track of them

    C. Building a raft

2. What are the three key elements of a Transaction?

    A. The sender, the receiver, and the amount

    B. The guardian, the asset, and the ledger

    C. The amount, the time, and the place

3. What is the role of validation in a Transaction?

    A. It builds a raft for the assets to travel on

    B. It ensures that the sender has enough assets and that the transaction is legitimate

    C. It adds decoration to the ledger

4. Why is recording Transactions in a ledger important?

    A. It helps everyone know who is playing games

    B. It keeps the system transparent and shows the updated ownership of assets

    C. It helps speed up the exchange process

5. How do Transactions support decentralized applications?

    A. They allow participants to interact and transact directly without needing a central authority

    B. They make the Wizard's magic stronger

    C. They create new keys for each transaction

Answers

1. **B** - A Transaction is compared to trading treasures and keeping track of them in a magical book.
2. **A** - The three key elements of a Transaction are the sender, the receiver, and the amount.
3. **B** - Validation ensures that the sender has enough assets and that the transaction is legitimate.
4. **B** - Recording Transactions in a ledger is important because it keeps the system transparent and shows the updated ownership of assets.

5. **A** - Transactions support decentralized applications by allowing participants to interact and transact directly without needing a central authority.

Unforgiving Marketplaces

A sudden burst of laughter erupted near the riverbank, where Robbie Rabbit, Pippa the playful panda, Barry Bear, and Kylie Kangaroo were gathered. Robbie had just finished a rather dramatic retelling of their last quest when a scroll fluttered down from the sky, landing softly in front of them.

Robbie's eyes sparkled with curiosity. "Looks like we have a new mission! Let's see what it's about."

Pippa tumbled forward and clapped her paws. "Read it, read it!"

Robbie unrolled the scroll and read aloud, "Today, we are to learn about different marketplaces: Centralized Exchange, OTC, and Dark Pools. We need to understand what they are and how they work!"

Barry tilted his head. "Marketplaces? That sounds fascinating."

Kylie nodded. "Let's head to the Wise Old Wizard's tower. He'll explain everything."

They made their way to the Wise Old Wizard's tower, where the Wizard greeted them warmly, his eyes twinkling with wisdom.

"Ah, Barry, Robbie, Kylie, and Pippa, welcome," the Wizard began. "Today, we will explore different types of marketplaces and understand their significance."

Kylie hopped in place. "What are these marketplaces, and how do they work?"

The Wizard nodded. "Imagine a bustling town square, a private trading room, and a secretive underground exchange. These scenarios represent different types of marketplaces in the digital realm (marketplaces)."

Robbie's ears perked up. "So, they're like places where we can trade treasures?"

"Exactly, Robbie," the Wizard replied. "Let's start with the Centralized Exchange. This is like a busy town square where everyone comes to trade their goods openly. There's a central authority, like the town mayor, who oversees all the trades and ensures everything runs smoothly (centralized control)."

With a wave of the Wizard's staff, a shimmering portal opened, leading them into a grand hall bustling with creatures trading enchanted items under the watchful eye of a town mayor.

"First, let's explore how Centralized Exchanges work," the Wizard said, leading them to a group of foxes and rabbits making trades. "On a Centralized Exchange, trades are facilitated by the central authority, which matches buyers and sellers and keeps records of all transactions (trade facilitation)."

Barry watched as the foxes and rabbits completed their trades. "So, the central authority makes sure all trades are fair?"

"Precisely, Barry," the Wizard replied. "Next, let's talk about Over-The-Counter (OTC) trades. This is like a private trading room where two parties negotiate and trade directly without involving the town mayor. It's used for larger or more discreet trades (private negotiation)."

They moved to another section of the hall where a group of squirrels were negotiating trades in a quiet room. "This process allows for flexibility and privacy, but it relies on the trust between the trading parties (trust and flexibility)," the Wizard explained.

Robbie hopped around the hall. "What about the secretive underground exchange?"

The Wizard smiled. "That brings us to Dark Pools. Imagine a hidden part of the marketplace where trades are made anonymously and privately. These trades are not visible to the public, providing an additional layer of secrecy (anonymity)."

They arrived at a dimly lit area where various creatures were making trades discreetly. "Dark Pools are used to trade large volumes without affecting the market price, but they lack the transparency of public exchanges (large volume trading)," the Wizard explained.

Pippa saw the creatures trading in the dimly lit area. "So, it's for those who want to keep their trades secret?"

"Exactly," the Wizard replied. "Now, let's talk about the benefits and drawbacks of each marketplace. Centralized Exchanges offer transparency and liquidity but can be vulnerable to hacking. OTC trades provide privacy and flexibility but require trust. Dark Pools offer anonymity and minimize market impact but lack transparency (pros and cons)."

Robbie clapped his paws. "This is amazing! What else?"

The Wizard nodded. "Understanding these marketplaces helps participants choose the best method for their trades based on their needs and preferences (market choice)."

Barry and Robbie spent the rest of the day exploring the different marketplaces, amazed by their structure, operation, and impact. Even Kylie and Pippa began to show interest, asking questions and engaging with the demonstrations. By the time the sun began to set, they felt enlightened and excited about the possibilities.

As they made their way back through the portal, Robbie couldn't help but make Barry, Kylie, and Pippa laugh with his impressions of the Wise Old Wizard explaining the marketplaces.

Barry, feeling wiser and more informed, knew that with the knowledge of these marketplaces, they could explore and trade in ways they had never imagined.

Explanation of Concepts

1. **Marketplaces**: Different types of digital marketplaces can be compared to a busy town square (Centralized Exchange), a private trading room (OTC), and a secretive underground exchange (Dark Pools). Each has unique characteristics and uses.
2. **Centralized Control**: A Centralized Exchange operates like a busy town square with a central authority overseeing trades. This central authority matches buyers and sellers, ensuring trades are fair and keeping records of all transactions.
3. **Trade Facilitation**: On a Centralized Exchange, the central authority facilitates trades, providing transparency and liquidity. However, centralized control can also make these exchanges vulnerable to hacking.
4. **Private Negotiation**: Over-The-Counter (OTC) trades occur in a private setting where two parties negotiate directly. This allows for flexibility and privacy but relies on the trust between the trading parties.
5. **Trust and Flexibility**: OTC trades provide the benefit of privacy and flexibility in negotiation but require trust between parties to ensure fair and successful trades.
6. **Anonymity**: Dark Pools offer a hidden part of the marketplace where trades are made anonymously and privately. This anonymity helps in trading large volumes without affecting the market price.
7. **Large Volume Trading**: Dark Pools are used to trade large volumes of assets discreetly, minimizing market

impact. However, they lack the transparency of public exchanges, which can pose risks.

8. **Pros and Cons**: Each marketplace has its benefits and drawbacks. Centralized Exchanges offer transparency and liquidity but are vulnerable to hacking. OTC trades provide privacy and flexibility but require trust. Dark Pools offer anonymity and minimize market impact but lack transparency.

9. **Market Choice**: Understanding the different marketplaces helps participants choose the best method for their trades based on their needs and preferences, whether they prioritize transparency, privacy, or anonymity.

Questions

1. What is a Centralized Exchange compared to in the story?

    A. A quiet room

    B. A hidden forest

    C. A busy town square

2. What is a key feature of Over-The-Counter (OTC) trades?

    A. They are overseen by a central authority

    B. They allow two parties to negotiate privately

    C. They are always made publicly

3. What is the purpose of Dark Pools in the marketplace?

    A. To trade large volumes of assets anonymously

    B. To allow public viewing of trades

    C. To only trade small amounts of items

4. What are some drawbacks of Centralized Exchanges?

    A. They lack transparency and liquidity

    B. They can be vulnerable to hacking

    C. They require trust between two parties

5. Why would someone choose to trade in a Dark Pool?

   A. To have complete transparency and public viewing

   B. To trade large volumes discreetly without affecting market prices

   C. To avoid private negotiations

Answers

1. **C** - A Centralized Exchange is compared to a busy town square where a central authority oversees trades.
2. **B** - Over-The-Counter (OTC) trades allow two parties to negotiate privately without involving a central authority.
3. **A** - Dark Pools are used to trade large volumes of assets anonymously, keeping the trades hidden from public view.
4. **B** - A drawback of Centralized Exchanges is that they can be vulnerable to hacking.
5. **B** - Someone would choose to trade in a Dark Pool to trade large volumes discreetly, minimizing market impact.

Liquid Pool of Treasures

A loud splash echoed through the forest as Pippa the playful panda attempted to catch a fish with her bare paws. Robbie Rabbit, with his feathered hat bouncing, burst through the bushes holding a scroll.

"Gather around, everyone! We've got a new quest!" Robbie announced with a grin.

Pippa tumbled over and clapped her paws. "What's it about this time, Robbie?"

"It's about something called a Liquidity Pool! We need to learn what it is and how it works!" Robbie said, his eyes gleaming with excitement.

"A Liquidity Pool? That sounds intriguing," Barry replied, setting down a log he had been carrying.

"Let's head to the Wise Old Wizard's tower. He'll explain everything," suggested Kylie Kangaroo.

They made their way to the Wise Old Wizard's tower, where the Wizard greeted them warmly, his eyes twinkling with wisdom.

"Ah, Barry, Robbie, Kylie, and Pippa, welcome," the Wizard began. "Today, we will explore the concept of a Liquidity Pool and understand its significance."

Kylie hopped in place. "What is a Liquidity Pool, and how does it work?"

The Wizard nodded. "Imagine a magical pond where everyone can contribute their treasures, and anyone can take what they need from it. This pond is replenished by the contributors and provides resources for everyone (shared resource)."

Robbie's ears perked up. "So, it's like a communal treasure chest?"

"Exactly, Robbie," the Wizard replied. "Let's start with the basics. A Liquidity Pool is a collection of funds from multiple participants that is used to facilitate trading and provide liquidity in a decentralized marketplace (collective funds)."

With a wave of the Wizard's staff, a shimmering portal opened, leading them into a grand hall filled with creatures contributing and withdrawing treasures from a large, enchanted pond.

"First, let's explore how Liquidity Pools work," the Wizard said, leading them to a group of foxes and rabbits adding and withdrawing items from the pond. "Participants contribute their assets to the pool, and in return, they receive a share of the pool's rewards (participant contribution)."

Barry watched as the foxes and rabbits completed their trades. "So, the contributors get rewarded for providing their treasures?"

"Precisely, Barry," the Wizard replied. "Next, let's talk about how these pools maintain balance. The value of assets in the pool is determined by an automated process that adjusts based on supply and demand (balance maintenance)."

They moved to another section of the hall where a group of squirrels were demonstrating the automated adjustments. "This process ensures that the pool remains balanced and fair, providing accurate pricing for trades (automated pricing)," the Wizard explained.

Robbie hopped around the hall. "What if someone wants to take out their contribution?"

The Wizard smiled. "Participants can withdraw their assets at any time, but the value they get back may vary based on the current state of the pool (withdrawal flexibility)."

They arrived at a station where a rabbit was demonstrating how to withdraw from the pool. "Withdrawing assets is straightforward, but the rewards and value depend on the pool's balance and the timing of the withdrawal (timing impact)," the Wizard explained.

Pippa saw the rabbit show how the pool worked. "So, the pool adjusts based on contributions and withdrawals?"

"Exactly," the Wizard replied. "Now, let's talk about the benefits of Liquidity Pools. They enable decentralized trading, reduce reliance on a single authority, and provide liquidity for various assets. This enhances the overall stability and efficiency of the market (decentralized benefits)."

Robbie clapped his paws. "This is amazing! What else?"

The Wizard nodded. "Liquidity Pools also support the development of decentralized applications and financial services, where participants can interact and trade directly with each other, fostering innovation and efficiency (decentralized applications)."

Barry and Robbie spent the rest of the day exploring the world of Liquidity Pools, amazed by their structure, operation, and impact. Even Kylie and Pippa began to show interest, asking questions and engaging with the demonstrations. By the time the sun began to set, they felt enlightened and excited about the possibilities.

As they made their way back through the portal, Robbie couldn't help but make Barry, Kylie, and Pippa laugh with his impressions of the Wise Old Wizard explaining Liquidity Pools.

Barry, feeling wiser and more informed, knew that with the knowledge of these technologies, they could explore and innovate in ways they had never imagined.

Explanation of Concepts

1. **Shared Resource**: A Liquidity Pool is like a communal treasure chest where everyone can contribute their assets. These pooled resources are available for trading and provide liquidity in a decentralized marketplace.
2. **Collective Funds**: Participants contribute their assets to the pool and receive a share of the pool's rewards. This encourages more contributions and maintains liquidity.
3. **Participant Contribution**: Contributors to the Liquidity Pool are rewarded based on their share of the total pool. This reward system incentivizes participation and helps maintain a healthy pool balance.
4. **Balance Maintenance**: The pool's value is maintained by an automated process that adjusts based on supply and demand. This ensures fair and accurate pricing for trades.
5. **Automated Pricing**: Automated systems adjust the value of assets in the pool, ensuring that the pool remains balanced and trades are executed at fair prices.
6. **Withdrawal Flexibility**: Participants can withdraw their assets from the pool at any time, but the value they receive may vary based on the pool's current state and the timing of the withdrawal.
7. **Timing Impact**: The rewards and value of withdrawn assets depend on the pool's balance and the timing of the withdrawal. Participants must consider these factors when deciding to withdraw.

8. **Decentralized Benefits**: Liquidity Pools enable decentralized trading, reduce reliance on a single authority, and provide liquidity for various assets. This enhances market stability and efficiency.
9. **Decentralized Applications**: Liquidity Pools support the development of decentralized applications and financial services, fostering innovation and allowing participants to trade directly with each other. This creates a more efficient and dynamic financial ecosystem.

Questions

1. What is a Liquidity Pool compared to in the story?

    A. A private vault

    B. A magical pond where treasures are shared

    C. A secret hideout

2. How do participants benefit from contributing to a Liquidity Pool?

    A. They receive nothing in return

    B. They are rewarded based on their share of the pool

    C. They lose their assets permanently

3. What helps maintain the balance of assets in the Liquidity Pool?

    A. A central authority

    B. Automated processes adjusting based on supply and demand

    C. Random chance

4. Can participants withdraw their assets from the Liquidity Pool, and does timing matter?

    A. Yes, they can withdraw at any time, and the timing affects the value they get

B. No, once contributed, assets cannot be withdrawn

C. They can withdraw anytime, but timing doesn't affect the value

5. What are the key benefits of Liquidity Pools in a decentralized marketplace?

A. They provide privacy for secret trades

B. They enable decentralized trading, reduce reliance on a single authority, and provide liquidity for various assets

C. They only allow small trades to occur

Answers

1. **B** - A Liquidity Pool is compared to a magical pond where treasures are shared by all and available for trading.
2. **B** - Participants are rewarded based on their share of the pool's total assets.
3. **B** - The balance is maintained by an automated process that adjusts the pool based on supply and demand.
4. **A** - Participants can withdraw their assets anytime, but the value they receive depends on the pool's state and timing.

5. **B** - Liquidity Pools enable decentralized trading, reduce reliance on a central authority, and provide liquidity for various assets, making the marketplace more efficient.

Case of the Magical Harvest

Raindrops drummed rhythmically on the leaves as the forest awoke to another lively day. A peculiar aroma filled the air, reminiscent of freshly baked bread and wildflowers. From behind a cluster of vibrant mushrooms, Robbie Rabbit hopped energetically, clutching a scroll that fluttered in the wind.

"Friends! Gather 'round!" Robbie announced, eyes sparkling with excitement.

Pippa the playful panda, rolling in the grass, giggled. "What's our mission today, Robbie?"

"It's something called Yield Farming! We need to learn what it is and how it works!" Robbie said, his voice brimming with enthusiasm.

"That sounds fascinating," Barry Bear replied, setting down a basket of honey.

"Let's head to the Wise Old Wizard's tower," suggested Kylie Kangaroo, bouncing up with curiosity.

They made their way through the forest to the Wise Old Wizard's tower, where the Wizard greeted them with a warm smile, his eyes filled with wisdom.

"Welcome, Barry, Robbie, Kylie, and Pippa," the Wizard began. "Today, we will explore the concept of Yield Farming and understand its significance."

Kylie hopped in place. "What is Yield Farming, and how does it work?"

The Wizard nodded. "Imagine a magical garden where you plant seeds, and in return, you receive a bountiful harvest. Yield Farming is like planting your digital assets in various DeFi platforms to earn rewards (harvesting rewards)."

Robbie's ears perked up. "So, it's like farming, but with treasures?"

"Exactly, Robbie," the Wizard replied. "Let's start with the basics. Yield Farming involves lending or staking your assets in a decentralized finance platform to earn interest or new tokens (earning interest)."

With a wave of the Wizard's staff, a shimmering portal opened, leading them into a grand garden filled with creatures tending to their crops.

"First, let's explore how Yield Farming works," the Wizard said, leading them to a group of foxes and rabbits planting and harvesting magical seeds. "Participants provide their assets to the platform, which then uses these assets to generate returns. The participants earn a share of these returns based on their contribution (participant returns)."

Barry watched as the foxes and rabbits tended to their crops. "So, they earn rewards based on how much they contribute?"

"Precisely, Barry," the Wizard replied. "Next, let's talk about the different strategies in Yield Farming. Some participants may choose to move their assets between multiple platforms to maximize their returns, a practice known as 'crop rotation' (strategy switching)."

They moved to another section of the garden where a group of squirrels were demonstrating the rotation of crops between different plots. "This strategy involves evaluating different platforms and moving assets to where they can earn the highest returns (platform evaluation)," the Wizard explained.

Robbie hopped around the garden. "What happens if the value of the crops changes?"

The Wizard smiled. "That brings us to the concept of 'Impermanent Loss'. When the value of your assets changes relative to when you first deposited them, you might end up with fewer assets than you started with if you withdraw at an unfavorable time (value fluctuation)."

They arrived at a station where a rabbit was demonstrating the impact of changing values on their crops. "Understanding the risks and timing your withdrawals carefully is crucial to minimizing losses (risk management)," the Wizard explained.

Pippa saw the rabbit demonstrate how the garden worked. "So, timing and understanding the value changes are important?"

"Exactly," the Wizard replied. "Now, let's talk about the benefits of Yield Farming. It allows participants to earn passive income on their digital assets, promotes liquidity in the market, and supports the growth of decentralized platforms (market liquidity)."

Robbie clapped his paws. "This is amazing! What else?"

The Wizard nodded. "Yield Farming also encourages innovation in the DeFi space, as platforms compete to offer better returns and attract more participants (innovation encouragement)."

Barry and Robbie spent the rest of the day exploring the world of Yield Farming, amazed by its structure, operation, and impact. Even Kylie and Pippa began to show interest, asking questions and engaging with the demonstrations. By the time the sun began to set, they felt enlightened and excited about the possibilities.

As they made their way back through the portal, Robbie couldn't help but make Barry, Kylie, and Pippa laugh with his impressions of the Wise Old Wizard explaining Yield Farming.

Barry, feeling wiser and more informed, knew that with the knowledge of these technologies, they could explore and innovate in ways they had never imagined.

Explanation of Concepts

1. **Harvesting Rewards**: Yield Farming is like planting your digital assets in various DeFi platforms to earn rewards. Just like a magical garden where planting seeds brings a bountiful harvest.
2. **Earning Interest**: In Yield Farming, participants lend or stake their assets on decentralized finance platforms. These platforms use the assets to generate returns, and participants earn a share of these returns based on their contributions.
3. **Participant Returns**: Participants provide their assets to the platform, which uses them to generate returns. The rewards earned are proportional to the amount contributed by each participant.
4. **Strategy Switching**: Some Yield Farmers move their assets between multiple platforms to maximize returns. This practice, known as 'crop rotation,' involves evaluating different platforms to find the best returns and adjusting the strategy accordingly.
5. **Platform Evaluation**: Successful Yield Farming often requires assessing different platforms to determine where assets can earn the highest returns. This might involve switching between platforms frequently to optimize earnings.
6. **Value Fluctuation**: 'Impermanent Loss' occurs when the value of deposited assets changes relative to their initial value. Participants may end up with fewer assets if they withdraw during an unfavorable market condition.

7. **Risk Management**: Understanding the risks and carefully timing withdrawals is crucial to minimize losses in Yield Farming. Effective risk management involves monitoring market conditions and adjusting strategies to mitigate potential losses.
8. **Market Liquidity**: Yield Farming provides liquidity to the market, which is essential for the efficient operation of decentralized platforms. It also allows participants to earn passive income on their digital assets.
9. **Innovation Encouragement**: Yield Farming fosters innovation in the DeFi space as platforms compete to offer better returns and attract more participants. This competition drives the development of new and improved financial products and services.

Questions

1. What is Yield Farming compared to in the story?

    A. A magic show

    B. Planting seeds in a magical garden to earn a harvest

    C. Building a castle

2. How do participants earn rewards in Yield Farming?

    A. By keeping their assets in a safe place

    B. By staking or lending their assets in decentralized finance platforms to generate returns

    C. By trading with other participants

3. What is 'crop rotation' in Yield Farming?

    A. Changing platforms to maximize returns by finding better opportunities

    B. Moving physical crops from one place to another

    C. Planting different seeds each time

4. What is Impermanent Loss?

    A. A type of bonus given to participants

B. A potential loss that happens when the value of deposited assets changes, leading to fewer assets when withdrawn at unfavorable times

C. A hidden treasure that appears randomly in the garden

5. What is one of the benefits of Yield Farming mentioned in the story?

A. It discourages people from participating in digital markets

B. It promotes market liquidity and supports the growth of decentralized platforms

C. It prevents any changes in asset values

Answers

1. **B** - Yield Farming is compared to planting seeds in a magical garden to earn a harvest.
2. **B** - Participants earn rewards by staking or lending their assets on decentralized finance platforms, which generate returns.
3. **A** - 'Crop rotation' in Yield Farming means changing platforms to find better opportunities and maximize returns.
4. **B** - Impermanent Loss refers to a potential loss that occurs when the value of deposited assets changes, affecting the final amount when withdrawn.

5. **B** - One benefit of Yield Farming is that it promotes market liquidity and supports the growth of decentralized platforms.

Stakes in the Evergreen Forest

Thunder rumbled faintly in the distance, and the air smelled of rain and freshly turned earth. A peculiar rustling in the bushes signaled the arrival of Robbie Rabbit, who burst into the clearing, clutching a scroll that shimmered with an iridescent glow.

"Gather 'round, everyone! We've got a new quest!" Robbie declared, his eyes twinkling with excitement.

Pippa the playful panda rolled over in the grass, clapping her paws. "What's it about this time, Robbie?"

Robbie unfurled the scroll and read aloud, "Today, we're to learn about something called Staking! We need to understand what it is and how it works!"

"That sounds intriguing," Barry Bear remarked, setting down a basket of berries.

"Let's head to the Wise Old Wizard's tower," suggested Kylie Kangaroo, bouncing up with eager curiosity.

The friends made their way through the forest to the Wise Old Wizard's tower. As they approached, the ancient wooden door creaked open, revealing the Wizard, his long beard glowing softly in the dim light.

"Ah, Barry, Robbie, Kylie, and Pippa, welcome," the Wizard greeted them warmly. "Today, we will delve into the wonders of Staking."

Kylie's ears twitched with anticipation. "What is Staking, and how does it work?"

The Wizard nodded thoughtfully. "Imagine a magical garden where enchanted seeds are planted, and in return, the gardener receives a portion of the garden's bounty. Staking is akin to this; you lock your digital assets in a network to earn rewards (reward earning)."

Robbie's ears perked up. "So, it's like farming, but with treasures?"

"Exactly, Robbie," the Wizard replied. "Staking involves locking up your assets to support the network's operations, and in return, you earn rewards (network support)."

With a flourish of his staff, the Wizard conjured a portal that transported them to a grand garden, teeming with activity. Creatures of all kinds were planting and harvesting magical seeds.

"Let's explore how Staking works," the Wizard said, leading them to a group of foxes and rabbits busily planting enchanted seeds. "Participants lock their assets in a staking contract, which helps secure the network and validate transactions. In return, they earn a share of the network's rewards (asset locking)."

Barry watched the foxes and rabbits tend to their magical crops. "So, the more they contribute, the more they earn?"

"Precisely, Barry," the Wizard affirmed. "Now, let's discuss different types of Staking. Some choose to stake individually, managing their own assets, while others join staking pools to combine resources and share the rewards (staking pools)."

They moved to another part of the garden, where squirrels were demonstrating both individual and pooled staking. "Individual staking requires more resources but offers greater control, while pooled staking allows participants to combine their resources and share rewards proportionally (resource combination)," the Wizard explained.

Robbie hopped excitedly. "What happens if someone wants to withdraw their stake?"

The Wizard smiled. "Participants can withdraw their staked assets, but there are often rules and penalties for early withdrawal, similar to how some magical contracts work (withdrawal penalties)."

They arrived at a demonstration where a rabbit was carefully explaining the process of withdrawing from a staking contract. "Timing is crucial, as withdrawing too soon can result in fewer rewards or penalties (timing impact)," the Wizard noted.

Pippa watched intently. "So, understanding the rules is important?"

"Exactly," the Wizard replied. "Now, let's talk about the benefits of Staking. It provides participants with a way to earn passive income, helps maintain the network's security, and supports the overall ecosystem's growth (ecosystem support)."

Robbie clapped his paws. "This is amazing! What else?"

The Wizard nodded. "Staking also fosters innovation in the DeFi space, as networks compete to offer better rewards and attract more participants (innovation encouragement)."

Barry and Robbie spent the rest of the day exploring the garden, marveling at its wonders. Even Kylie and Pippa grew more curious, asking questions and engaging with the demonstrations. By sunset, they felt enlightened and excited about the possibilities.

As they made their way back through the portal, Robbie couldn't resist mimicking the Wise Old Wizard's serious tone, causing Barry, Kylie, and Pippa to laugh.

Barry, feeling wiser and more informed, knew that with the knowledge of these technologies, they could explore and innovate in ways they had never imagined.

Explanation of Concepts

1. **Reward Earning**: Staking is like planting enchanted seeds in a magical garden, where participants lock their digital assets to earn rewards. This is akin to receiving a portion of the garden's bounty.
2. **Network Support**: By staking, participants lock up their assets to support the network's operations. This helps secure the network and validate transactions, ensuring its stability and security.
3. **Asset Locking**: Participants lock their assets in a staking contract, contributing to the network's security. In return, they earn a share of the network's rewards based on their contribution.
4. **Staking Pools**: Some participants choose to stake individually, managing their assets and rewards. Others join staking pools, combining their resources to share rewards proportionally, making it accessible to those with fewer resources.
5. **Resource Combination**: Combining resources in a staking pool allows participants to share rewards proportionally. This approach offers a way to participate in staking without needing large amounts of assets.
6. **Withdrawal Penalties**: Participants can withdraw their staked assets, but early withdrawal may result in penalties. Understanding the rules and timing withdrawals correctly is crucial to maximize rewards.
7. **Timing Impact**: Timing is essential in staking, as withdrawing assets too soon can result in fewer rewards

or penalties. Participants must carefully consider the timing of their withdrawals.
8. **Ecosystem Support**: Staking provides a way to earn passive income and helps maintain the network's security. It also supports the overall growth and health of the ecosystem.
9. **Innovation Encouragement**: Staking fosters innovation in the DeFi space, as networks compete to offer better rewards and attract more participants. This competition drives the development of new and improved financial products and services.

Questions

1. What is Staking compared to in the story?

    A. Building a castle

    B. Planting enchanted seeds in a magical garden to earn rewards

    C. Catching fish in a pond

2. What do participants do with their assets when they stake them?

    A. Spend them

    B. Lock them up to support the network's operations and earn rewards

    C. Hide them from others

3. What is the purpose of a staking pool?

    A. A place to swim

    B. A group of participants combining their assets to share rewards proportionally

    C. A magical garden where only one person can participate

4. What happens if someone withdraws their staked assets too early?

    A. They receive bonus rewards

B. They might face penalties or receive fewer rewards

C. They double their rewards

5. How does staking benefit the overall ecosystem?

   A. It helps participants relax

   B. It provides passive income, supports network security, and promotes ecosystem growth

   C. It allows participants to sell their assets quickly

Answers

1. **B** - Staking is compared to planting enchanted seeds in a magical garden to earn rewards.
2. **B** - Participants lock their assets to support the network's operations and earn rewards.
3. **B** - A staking pool is where participants combine their assets to share rewards proportionally.
4. **B** - If someone withdraws their staked assets too early, they may face penalties or receive fewer rewards.
5. **B** - Staking provides passive income, supports network security, and promotes ecosystem growth.

Blockchain Bedtime Stories

Lending Library of Evergreen Forest

A cool breeze rustled the leaves of Evergreen Forest as a peculiar golden glow settled over the clearing. The curious friends—Barry Bear, Robbie Rabbit, Pippa the playful panda, and Kylie Kangaroo—noticed the glow emanating from a mysterious scroll lying near the brook.

"Gather 'round, everyone! This looks important!" Robbie Rabbit exclaimed, his nose twitching with excitement.

Pippa somersaulted over, clapping her paws. "What's it about this time, Robbie?"

Robbie unrolled the scroll and read aloud, "Today, we're to learn about Collateral and Lending/Borrowing in the magical world of DeFi!"

"That sounds intriguing," Barry Bear remarked, setting down his honey jar.

"Let's head to the Wise Old Wizard's tower," suggested Kylie Kangaroo, her ears perking up with curiosity.

The friends made their way to the Wise Old Wizard's tower. The Wizard greeted them with a warm smile, his eyes gleaming with wisdom.

"Welcome, Barry, Robbie, Kylie, and Pippa," the Wizard began. "Today, we'll explore the enchanted concepts of Collateral and Lending/Borrowing."

Kylie bounced on her feet. "What are these concepts, and how do they work?"

The Wizard nodded thoughtfully. "Imagine a magical library where you can borrow any enchanted book, but you must leave something valuable behind as a promise to return it. That valuable item is your Collateral (collateral)."

Robbie's ears twitched. "So, it's like giving a treasure to borrow a book?"

"Exactly, Robbie," the Wizard replied. "Collateral is something of value that you pledge to secure a loan. If you fail to return what you borrowed, the lender keeps the collateral (security)."

With a flick of his staff, the Wizard conjured a portal that transported them to a grand library filled with magical books and artifacts.

"First, let's explore how Collateral works," the Wizard said, leading them to a group of foxes and rabbits trading enchanted items for books. "Participants offer their treasures as collateral to borrow enchanted books. The value of the collateral must match or exceed the value of the borrowed item (value matching)."

Barry watched the foxes and rabbits carefully. "So, they have to leave something valuable to ensure they return the book?"

"Precisely, Barry," the Wizard affirmed. "Now, let's talk about Lending and Borrowing. When someone needs an enchanted book but doesn't have the necessary item, they can borrow it by offering collateral. In return, they promise to return the book and pay a small fee (borrowing fee)."

They moved to another section of the library where squirrels were borrowing books. "Lending and borrowing allow creatures to access resources they need without permanently giving up their treasures (resource access)," the Wizard explained.

Robbie hopped around the library. "What happens if someone can't return the book?"

The Wizard smiled. "If the borrower fails to return the book, the lender keeps the collateral as compensation. This ensures that lenders are protected from losses (lender protection)."

They arrived at a demonstration where a rabbit explained the consequences of failing to return a borrowed book. "Understanding the risks and ensuring you can meet your obligations is crucial in lending and borrowing (risk management)," the Wizard noted.

Pippa watched intently. "So, it's important to know what you're promising?"

"Exactly," the Wizard replied. "Now, let's discuss the benefits of Collateral and Lending/Borrowing. These practices provide access to needed resources, encourage responsible borrowing, and ensure a fair system for everyone (system fairness)."

Robbie clapped his paws. "This is amazing! What else?"

The Wizard nodded. "These practices also foster trust within the community, as everyone knows that their treasures are secure and they can access what they need (community trust)."

Barry and Robbie spent the rest of the day exploring the enchanted library, amazed by its wonders. Even Kylie and Pippa grew more curious, asking questions and engaging with the demonstrations. By sunset, they felt enlightened and excited about the possibilities.

As they made their way back through the portal, Robbie couldn't resist mimicking the Wise Old Wizard's serious tone, causing Barry, Kylie, and Pippa to laugh.

Barry, feeling wiser and more informed, knew that with the knowledge of these practices, they could explore and innovate in ways they had never imagined.

Explanation of Concepts

1. **Collateral**: Collateral is something valuable that a borrower pledges to secure a loan. If the borrower fails to repay the loan, the lender keeps the collateral. This concept ensures the lender is protected from losses and encourages responsible borrowing.
2. **Security**: When you borrow something valuable, you must provide collateral as security. This ensures that if you fail to return what you borrowed, the lender can keep the collateral as compensation.
3. **Value Matching**: The value of the collateral must match or exceed the value of the borrowed item. This ensures that the lender is adequately compensated in case the borrower fails to return the item.
4. **Borrowing Fee**: Borrowers pay a small fee to access the resources they need. This fee compensates the lender for the temporary use of their asset and provides an incentive for lending.
5. **Resource Access**: Lending and borrowing allow individuals to access resources without permanently giving up their treasures. This system provides flexibility and ensures that resources are used efficiently.
6. **Lender Protection**: If a borrower fails to return the borrowed item, the lender keeps the collateral. This protection ensures that lenders are not at a loss and encourages a fair and trustworthy system.
7. **Risk Management**: Understanding the risks involved and ensuring that obligations can be met is crucial in

lending and borrowing. Proper risk management protects both the borrower and the lender.
8. **System Fairness**: The practices of collateral and lending/borrowing ensure a fair system where borrowers can access needed resources, and lenders are compensated for their risk.
9. **Community Trust**: These practices foster trust within the community, as everyone knows their treasures are secure and they can access resources when needed. This trust encourages cooperation and mutual benefit.

Questions

1. What is Collateral in the story compared to?

    A. A magical book

    B. A treasure left behind as a promise to return a borrowed item

    C. A sparkling gem in the forest

2. Why do borrowers need to offer Collateral when borrowing something?

    A. To show their wealth

    B. To ensure the lender is protected if the borrower doesn't return the item

    C. To make the borrowing process more fun

3. What happens if the borrower fails to return the borrowed item?

    A. The borrower gets more time to return the item

    B. The lender keeps the collateral as compensation

    C. The item magically disappears

4. What is the benefit of Lending and Borrowing in the enchanted library?

    A. It allows creatures to access resources without permanently giving up their treasures

B. It makes the library more magical

C. It allows everyone to keep the borrowed books forever

5. Why is understanding the risks important when borrowing something?

A. Because it's fun to take risks

B. It ensures that both the borrower and lender are protected, and obligations can be met

C. So the borrower can borrow even more items in the future

Answers

1. **B** - Collateral is compared to a treasure left behind as a promise to return a borrowed item.
2. **B** - Borrowers offer Collateral to ensure the lender is protected if the item isn't returned.
3. **B** - If the borrower fails to return the item, the lender keeps the collateral as compensation.
4. **A** - Lending and borrowing allow creatures to access resources without permanently giving up their treasures.
5. **B** - Understanding the risks ensures both parties are protected, and obligations can be met.

Leaf it to Us

The forest was unusually quiet, with a strange shimmering light coming from the grove near the old oak tree. It was here that the friends—Barry Bear, Robbie Rabbit, Pippa the playful panda, and Kylie Kangaroo—gathered around a peculiar glowing seed they had found on their morning walk.

"This seed looks special," Kylie remarked, her eyes wide with curiosity.

"Let's take it to the Wise Old Wizard. He'll know what to do with it," suggested Robbie, his nose twitching excitedly.

They made their way to the Wise Old Wizard's tower, where the Wizard greeted them with a warm smile, his eyes twinkling with wisdom.

"Welcome, Barry, Robbie, Kylie, and Pippa," the Wizard began. "I see you've found the enchanted seed. This seed will help us explore the concept of a Merkle Tree."

Pippa tumbled forward, giggling. "A Merkle Tree? What's that?"

The Wizard nodded. "Imagine a magical tree that helps keep track of all the enchanted items in the forest, ensuring they are all accounted for and none are lost or duplicated. This tree is called a Merkle Tree (data structure)."

Robbie's ears perked up. "So, it's like a ledger for all the forest's treasures?"

"Exactly, Robbie," the Wizard replied. "Let's start with the basics. A Merkle Tree is a way to organize and verify large sets of data efficiently. Each leaf or node of the tree contains a piece of data, and branches are created by combining and hashing these data pieces (organize and verify)."

With a wave of his staff, the Wizard conjured an image of a tree with glowing leaves and branches. "Each leaf on this tree represents a piece of data, and the branches combine these data points into a single root, called the Merkle Root (Merkle Root)."

Barry watched the tree carefully. "So, how does this help keep everything organized?"

The Wizard smiled. "The Merkle Root is a unique fingerprint of all the data in the tree. If even a single piece of data changes, the Merkle Root changes too. This helps verify the integrity of the data without having to check every individual piece (data integrity)."

They moved closer to the glowing tree, where small creatures were placing enchanted items on the leaves. "These items are like the data pieces in the Merkle Tree. As each item is added, it's combined with another and hashed to form a branch. This continues until all branches lead to the single Merkle Root (hashing process)," the Wizard explained.

Robbie hopped around the tree. "What happens if someone tries to change an item?"

The Wizard pointed to a glowing leaf. "If an item is changed, its hash changes, which affects the hash of the branch it's part of, and so on up to the Merkle Root. This makes it easy to detect any tampering or errors (tamper detection)."

Pippa saw the creatures carefully placing and hashing the items. "So, it's really important for keeping everything secure and accurate?"

"Exactly," the Wizard replied. "Now, let's discuss the benefits of the Merkle Tree. It allows for efficient and secure verification of data, reduces the need to store large amounts of data, and ensures data integrity (benefits)."

Robbie clapped his paws. "This is amazing! What else?"

The Wizard nodded. "The Merkle Tree also enables fast and secure transactions, as verifying data integrity is quick and doesn't require checking each piece individually. This makes it ideal for use in complex systems like blockchain (fast verification)."

Barry and Robbie spent the rest of the day exploring the enchanted tree, amazed by its structure, operation, and impact. Even Kylie and Pippa grew more curious, asking questions and engaging with the demonstrations. By sunset, they felt enlightened and excited about the possibilities.

As they made their way back through the forest, Robbie couldn't resist mimicking the Wise Old Wizard's serious tone, causing Barry, Kylie, and Pippa to laugh.

Barry, feeling wiser and more informed, knew that with the knowledge of these technologies, they could explore and innovate in ways they had never imagined.

Explanation of Concepts

1. **Data Structure**: A Merkle Tree is a structure used to organize and verify large sets of data efficiently. It ensures all data is accounted for and none is lost or duplicated, making it like a ledger for digital information.
2. **Organize and Verify**: Each leaf or node in a Merkle Tree contains a piece of data. Branches are formed by combining and hashing these data pieces, creating an organized and verifiable structure.
3. **Merkle Root**: The Merkle Root is the unique fingerprint of all the data in the tree. It's the single point at the top of the tree that represents the combined hashes of all data, ensuring data integrity and verification.
4. **Data Integrity**: The Merkle Root helps verify the integrity of the data without checking every individual piece. If even a single piece of data changes, the Merkle Root changes, making it easy to detect tampering or errors.
5. **Hashing Process**: The process of combining and hashing data pieces into branches and eventually the Merkle Root. This secure method ensures that changes in data are easily detectable, maintaining data accuracy and security.
6. **Tamper Detection**: If any data is altered, its hash changes, affecting the entire branch up to the Merkle Root. This makes it easy to detect any tampering or errors, ensuring the security of the data.

7. **Benefits**: The Merkle Tree allows for efficient and secure verification of data, reduces the need to store large amounts of data, and ensures data integrity. It's essential for maintaining accurate and secure data records.
8. **Fast Verification**: Verifying data integrity in a Merkle Tree is quick and doesn't require checking each piece individually. This makes it ideal for use in complex systems like blockchain, where fast and secure transactions are necessary.

Questions

1. What does the Merkle Tree help with in the enchanted forest?

    A. Growing magical plants

    B. Keeping track of all enchanted items and ensuring none are lost or duplicated

    C. Creating new enchanted items

2. What is the Merkle Root in the Merkle Tree?

    A. The tree's oldest root

    B. A unique fingerprint that represents all the combined data in the tree

    C. A glowing branch that changes colors

3. What happens if someone changes an enchanted item on the tree?

    A. The tree grows a new branch

    B. The hash of the item changes, affecting the entire branch up to the Merkle Root

    C. The tree starts to glow brighter

4. Why is the hashing process important in the Merkle Tree?

    A. It makes the tree grow faster

B. It ensures that changes in data are easily detectable, keeping the data accurate and secure

C. It turns the data into treasure

5. What is one of the benefits of using a Merkle Tree for data?

A. It reduces the need to store large amounts of data and ensures quick, secure verification

B. It helps create more space for storing treasures

C. It makes the data invisible to everyone

Answers

1. **B** - The Merkle Tree helps keep track of all enchanted items and ensures none are lost or duplicated.
2. **B** - The Merkle Root is a unique fingerprint that represents all the combined data in the tree.
3. **B** - If someone changes an enchanted item, the hash of the item changes, affecting the entire branch up to the Merkle Root.
4. **B** - The hashing process ensures that changes in data are easily detectable, keeping the data accurate and secure.

5. **A** - One of the benefits of the Merkle Tree is reducing the need to store large amounts of data and ensuring quick, secure verification.

Fuel for Thought

A peculiar humming sound filled the air as Barry Bear, Robbie Rabbit, Pippa the playful panda, and Kylie Kangaroo gathered in the clearing. Robbie, always the first to investigate, found a mysterious bottle with a glowing blue liquid inside.

"This looks interesting," Robbie exclaimed, his nose twitching with excitement.

"Let's take it to the Wise Old Wizard. He'll know what it is," suggested Kylie, her eyes wide with curiosity.

They made their way to the Wise Old Wizard's tower, where the Wizard greeted them with a warm smile, his eyes twinkling with wisdom.

"Welcome, Barry, Robbie, Kylie, and Pippa," the Wizard began. "I see you've found the Bottle of Enchanted Gwei. Today, we'll explore its mysteries."

Pippa tumbled forward, giggling. "What is Gwei?"

The Wizard nodded. "Imagine you need to light a series of magical lamps, but each lamp requires a small amount of a special liquid to work. This liquid is called Gwei, and it powers the lamps. In the world of Ethereum, Gwei is used to pay for transactions and computations (small units of value)."

Robbie's ears perked up. "So, it's like fuel for the lamps?"

"Exactly, Robbie," the Wizard replied. "Let's start with the basics. Gwei is a small unit of measure, like drops of this liquid, used to pay for the computational work required to perform actions in the Ethereum network (transaction fee)."

With a wave of his staff, the Wizard conjured an image of a grand hall filled with glowing lamps, each one requiring a drop of the enchanted liquid to shine brightly.

"First, let's explore how Gwei works," the Wizard said, leading them to the glowing lamps. "Each action you want to perform in the Ethereum network, like sending a message or casting a spell, requires a certain amount of computational work. This work is measured in gas, and the cost of the gas is paid in Gwei (computational cost)."

Barry watched the lamps carefully. "So, the more complex the action, the more Gwei you need?"

"Precisely, Barry," the Wizard affirmed. "Now, let's talk about the Gas Limit and Gas Price. The Gas Limit is the maximum amount of gas you're willing to use for an action, while the Gas Price is how much you're willing to pay per unit of gas (gas limit and price)."

They moved closer to a lamp where a fox was adjusting the flow of the enchanted liquid. "Setting a higher Gas Price can make your actions happen faster, but it costs more Gwei. Setting a lower Gas Price saves Gwei but may take longer (transaction speed)," the Wizard explained.

Robbie hopped around the lamps. "What happens if I run out of Gwei before the action is completed?"

The Wizard smiled. "If you run out of Gwei, the action stops, but you still have to pay for the gas used up until that point. It's important to set your Gas Limit high enough to complete the action (insufficient gas)."

They arrived at a demonstration where a rabbit was carefully setting the Gas Limit and Gas Price for lighting a series of lamps. "Understanding how to set these limits helps ensure your actions are completed efficiently and within your budget (efficiency and budgeting)," the Wizard noted.

Pippa watched intently. "So, it's really important to manage your Gwei wisely?"

"Exactly," the Wizard replied. "Now, let's discuss the benefits of Gwei and gas in the Ethereum network. They ensure that everyone pays their fair share for using the network, prevent abuse by making it costly to perform meaningless actions, and help maintain the network's efficiency and security (network security)."

Robbie clapped his paws. "This is amazing! What else?"

The Wizard nodded. "Using Gwei and gas also encourages developers to write efficient code, as less complex actions cost less Gwei. This fosters innovation and keeps the network running smoothly (developer efficiency)."

Barry and Robbie spent the rest of the day exploring the enchanted lamps, amazed by their operation and impact. Even Kylie and Pippa grew more curious, asking questions and engaging with the demonstrations. By sunset, they felt enlightened and excited about the possibilities.

As they made their way back through the forest, Robbie couldn't resist mimicking the Wise Old Wizard's serious tone, causing Barry, Kylie, and Pippa to laugh.

Barry, feeling wiser and more informed, knew that with the knowledge of these technologies, they could explore and innovate in ways they had never imagined.

Explanation of Concepts

1. **Small Units of Value**: Gwei is a small unit of measure used in the Ethereum network to pay for computational work. It's like drops of enchanted liquid used to power magical lamps, with each drop representing a small amount of value.
2. **Transaction Fee**: In the Ethereum network, each action requires computational work, and the cost of this work is measured in gas. Gwei is used to pay for this gas, making it the fuel that powers transactions and computations.
3. **Computational Cost**: The more complex an action, the more gas it requires. The cost of this gas, paid in Gwei, reflects the computational resources needed to perform the action. Setting the right Gas Limit and Gas Price ensures the action can be completed efficiently.
4. **Gas Limit and Price**: The Gas Limit is the maximum amount of gas you're willing to use for an action, while the Gas Price is how much you're willing to pay per unit of gas. Higher Gas Prices can make actions happen faster but cost more Gwei, while lower Gas Prices save Gwei but may take longer.
5. **Transaction Speed**: Setting a higher Gas Price can expedite actions in the Ethereum network, as it signals to the network that you're willing to pay more for faster processing. Balancing speed and cost is crucial for efficient transactions.
6. **Insufficient Gas**: If you run out of Gwei before an action is completed, the action stops, but you still pay

for the gas used up until that point. Setting your Gas Limit high enough is essential to avoid incomplete actions and wasted Gwei.

7. **Efficiency and Budgeting**: Managing your Gwei wisely involves setting appropriate Gas Limits and Gas Prices to ensure actions are completed efficiently and within your budget. This helps prevent overspending and incomplete transactions.
8. **Network Security**: Gwei and gas ensure that users pay their fair share for using the Ethereum network, preventing abuse by making it costly to perform meaningless actions. This maintains the network's efficiency and security.
9. **Developer Efficiency**: The use of Gwei and gas encourages developers to write efficient code, as less complex actions cost less Gwei. This fosters innovation and helps keep the Ethereum network running smoothly.

Questions

1. What is Gwei in the Ethereum network?

    A. A magical animal

    B. A small unit of measure used to pay for computational work

    C. A type of food for enchanted creatures

2. What happens if you set a higher Gas Price when performing an action on the Ethereum network?

    A. The action will cost more Gwei but may happen faster

    B. The action will take longer to complete

    C. The action will not work at all

3. What is the Gas Limit?

    A. The minimum amount of Gwei you can use for an action

    B. The maximum amount of gas you're willing to use for an action

    C. A magical potion that makes your actions free

4. What happens if you run out of Gwei before your action is completed?

A. The action stops, and you still pay for the gas used up until that point

B. The action continues and completes for free

C. The action fails, but you don't lose any Gwei

5. Why is it important to manage your Gwei wisely when performing actions in the Ethereum network?

A. To avoid overspending and incomplete transactions

B. To make sure you never use Gwei

C. To impress the Wise Old Wizard

Answers

1. **B** - Gwei is a small unit of measure used to pay for computational work in the Ethereum network.
2. **A** - Setting a higher Gas Price can make the action happen faster, but it will cost more Gwei.
3. **B** - The Gas Limit is the maximum amount of gas you're willing to use for an action.
4. **A** - If you run out of Gwei before the action is completed, the action stops, and you still pay for the gas used up until that point.
5. **A** - Managing your Gwei wisely helps avoid overspending and incomplete transactions.

Quest for Satoshi's Treasure

A mysterious map floated down from the sky, carried by a playful breeze. It landed right in the middle of the clearing where Barry Bear, Robbie Rabbit, Pippa the playful panda, and Kylie Kangaroo were enjoying a picnic.

"Look at this!" Robbie exclaimed, holding up the map. "It's an invitation to find Satoshi's Treasure!"

Kylie's ears twitched with curiosity. "Who's Satoshi, and what's his treasure?"

"The Wise Old Wizard will know!" suggested Pippa, rolling to her feet.

Together, they made their way through the forest to the Wise Old Wizard's tower. The Wizard greeted them warmly, his eyes twinkling with a hint of mischief.

"Ah, you've found the map to Satoshi's Treasure," the Wizard said, his voice filled with excitement. "Today, we'll uncover the secrets of Bitcoin and learn about 'Sats' and 'Satoshi'."

Robbie's nose twitched. "What are Sats and Satoshi?"

The Wizard nodded. "Imagine a giant, magical gold coin called Bitcoin. This coin is so valuable that it's divided into tiny pieces to make trading easier. These tiny pieces are called Sats, short for Satoshi, named after the mysterious creator of Bitcoin (small units of value)."

Pippa giggled. "So, it's like breaking a big cookie into crumbs to share with everyone?"

"Exactly, Pippa," the Wizard replied. "Each Bitcoin is made up of 100 million Sats. This allows people to trade even the smallest portions of Bitcoin, making it accessible to everyone (divisibility)."

With a wave of his staff, the Wizard conjured a shimmering portal that transported them to a vast treasure chamber filled with golden coins, each labeled with numbers and glowing softly.

"First, let's explore the concept of Sats," the Wizard said, leading them to a massive gold coin. "This coin represents one Bitcoin. When divided into Sats, it's easier to trade and use, just like having smaller denominations of currency (currency)."

Barry watched the glowing coins carefully. "So, each Sat is a tiny part of a Bitcoin?"

"Precisely, Barry," the Wizard affirmed. "Now, let's talk about Satoshi Nakamoto, the enigmatic creator of Bitcoin. No one knows who Satoshi really is, but his creation has revolutionized the world of digital currency (mystery)."

The Origins of Bitcoin

The Wizard led them to a grand tapestry depicting the history of Bitcoin. "In 2008, someone using the pseudonym Satoshi Nakamoto published a paper describing a new form of digital money called Bitcoin. The idea was to create a decentralized currency, free from the control of any government or institution (decentralized currency)."

Robbie's eyes widened. "So, Bitcoin isn't controlled by anyone?"

"Exactly," the Wizard replied. "Bitcoin transactions are verified by a network of computers, called nodes, that work together to ensure the accuracy and security of the transactions. This process is known as mining (mining)."

Kylie bounced on her feet. "What's mining?"

The Wizard smiled. "Mining is the process of validating and recording transactions on the blockchain. Miners use powerful computers to solve complex mathematical problems, and the first one to solve the problem gets to add the transaction to the blockchain and is rewarded with new Bitcoins (blockchain, reward)."

Understanding Sats and Bitcoin Transactions

They moved closer to a display where holograms of Bitcoin transactions floated in the air. "Bitcoin transactions are recorded on a public ledger called the blockchain, ensuring transparency and security. Each transaction can involve fractions of a Bitcoin, often measured in Sats (transactions)," the Wizard explained.

Robbie hopped around the holograms. "What happens if I want to send someone a small amount of Bitcoin?"

The Wizard smiled. "You can send any amount, even just a few Sats. This flexibility makes Bitcoin useful for a wide range of transactions, from large purchases to small tips (flexibility)."

They arrived at a demonstration where a rabbit showed how to send and receive Sats using a magical ledger. "Understanding how to manage and use Sats is crucial for participating in the Bitcoin network efficiently (management)," the Wizard noted.

Pippa watched intently. "So, it's really important to know how to handle Sats and Bitcoin?"

"Exactly," the Wizard replied. "Now, let's discuss the benefits of using Sats and Bitcoin. They provide a decentralized way to transfer value, free from traditional banking systems, and enable quick, secure transactions (decentralization)."

Robbie clapped his paws. "This is amazing! What else?"

The Wizard nodded. "Bitcoin also encourages financial inclusion, allowing people around the world to participate in the global economy without needing a bank account (inclusion)."

Barry and Robbie spent the rest of the day exploring the treasure chamber, amazed by its wonders. Even Kylie and Pippa grew more curious, asking questions and engaging with the demonstrations. By sunset, they felt enlightened and excited about the possibilities.

As they made their way back through the portal, Robbie couldn't resist mimicking the Wise Old Wizard's serious tone, causing Barry, Kylie, and Pippa to laugh.

Barry, feeling wiser and more informed, knew that with the knowledge of these technologies, they could explore and innovate in ways they had never imagined.

Explanation of Concepts

1. **Small Units of Value**: Sats, short for Satoshi, are tiny pieces of Bitcoin. Each Bitcoin is divided into 100 million Sats, making it easier to trade and use. This is like breaking a big cookie into crumbs to share with everyone.
2. **Divisibility**: Dividing Bitcoin into smaller units, like Sats, allows people to trade even the smallest portions. This makes Bitcoin accessible to everyone and enables a wide range of transactions.
3. **Currency**: Bitcoin can be compared to a giant, magical gold coin. Dividing it into Sats makes it easier to trade, similar to having smaller denominations of traditional currency.
4. **Mystery**: Satoshi Nakamoto is the mysterious creator of Bitcoin. His creation has revolutionized digital currency, but no one knows his true identity. This adds an element of intrigue to Bitcoin's history.
5. **Transactions**: Bitcoin transactions are recorded on a public ledger called the blockchain. Each transaction can involve fractions of a Bitcoin, measured in Sats. This ensures transparency and security in the Bitcoin network.
6. **Flexibility**: Bitcoin's divisibility allows for flexible transactions. You can send any amount, even just a few Sats, making it useful for various purposes, from large purchases to small tips.
7. **Management**: Understanding how to manage and use Sats is crucial for efficiently participating in the Bitcoin

network. This involves knowing how to send and receive Sats using digital ledgers.

8. **Decentralization**: Using Sats and Bitcoin provides a decentralized way to transfer value, free from traditional banking systems. This enables quick, secure transactions without the need for intermediaries.
9. **Inclusion**: Bitcoin encourages financial inclusion by allowing people worldwide to participate in the global economy without needing a bank account. This opens up opportunities for financial participation to those who may not have access to traditional banking services.
10. **Mining**: Mining is the process of validating and recording Bitcoin transactions on the blockchain. Miners use powerful computers to solve complex mathematical problems, and the first one to solve the problem gets to add the transaction to the blockchain and is rewarded with new Bitcoins. This ensures the security and accuracy of the Bitcoin network.
11. **Blockchain**: The blockchain is a public ledger where all Bitcoin transactions are recorded. It ensures transparency and security, as each transaction is verified by a network of nodes working together. This makes it difficult for any single entity to manipulate the data.

Questions

1. What are Sats in the context of Bitcoin?

    A. A type of animal

    B. Small units of Bitcoin

    C. A magic potion

2. Why is Bitcoin divided into smaller units like Sats?

    A. To make it easier to trade and use smaller portions

    B. To make it more difficult to trade

    C. To hide the value of Bitcoin

3. Who is Satoshi Nakamoto?

    A. A famous wizard

    B. The mysterious creator of Bitcoin

    C. A type of digital coin

4. What is mining in the Bitcoin network?

    A. Digging for gold in the forest

    B. The process of validating and recording Bitcoin transactions

    C. A way to divide Bitcoin into smaller pieces

5. How does Bitcoin promote financial inclusion?

   A. By allowing people to trade only large amounts

   B. By requiring a bank account for all transactions

   C. By enabling people worldwide to participate in the economy without needing a bank account

Answers

1. **B** - Sats are small units of Bitcoin, making it easier to trade smaller portions.
2. **A** - Bitcoin is divided into smaller units like Sats to make it more accessible and easier to use in smaller transactions.
3. **B** - Satoshi Nakamoto is the mysterious creator of Bitcoin, whose identity remains unknown.
4. **B** - Mining is the process of validating and recording Bitcoin transactions on the blockchain, ensuring the network's security.
5. **C** - Bitcoin promotes financial inclusion by allowing people around the world to participate in the global economy without needing a traditional bank account.

Bear with Blockchains

A soft breeze carried the sweet scent of wildflowers through Evergreen Forest. A sudden burst of light caught the attention of Barry Bear, Robbie Rabbit, Pippa the playful panda, and Kylie Kangaroo. They gathered around the source of the glow—a shimmering crystal embedded in the forest floor.

"Look at this!" Robbie Rabbit exclaimed, his nose twitching with curiosity. "I wonder what it is."

"Let's take it to the Wise Old Wizard," suggested Kylie, her eyes wide with excitement. "He'll know what to do."

The friends made their way to the Wise Old Wizard's tower. The Wizard greeted them with a warm smile, his eyes gleaming with wisdom.

"Welcome, Barry, Robbie, Kylie, and Pippa," the Wizard began. "I see you've found the Crystal of Clarity. Today, we'll explore the concept of Public and Private Blockchains."

Pippa tumbled forward, giggling. "What are Public and Private Blockchains?"

The Wizard nodded. "Imagine two enchanted ledgers. One is open for everyone to see and contribute to, while the other is restricted to a select group. These ledgers represent Public and Private Blockchains (types of blockchains)."

Robbie's ears perked up. "So, it's like an open book and a private diary?"

"Exactly, Robbie," the Wizard replied. "Let's start with the basics. A blockchain is a digital ledger that records transactions in a secure and immutable way. Each entry, or block, is linked to the previous one, forming a chain (digital ledger)."

With a wave of his staff, the Wizard conjured an image of two books—one glowing with an open aura, and the other protected by a magical lock.

"First, let's explore Public Blockchains," the Wizard said, pointing to the open book. "These blockchains are accessible to anyone. They are decentralized, meaning no single entity controls them, and they rely on a network of participants to validate transactions (decentralized validation)."

Barry watched the open book carefully. "So, anyone can join and help keep it running?"

"Precisely, Barry," the Wizard affirmed. "Public blockchains are transparent and secure, but they can be slower and require more resources to maintain (transparency and security)."

They moved closer to the glowing open book, where small creatures were adding and validating entries. "In a Public Blockchain, anyone can participate in the validation process, making it highly secure but sometimes less efficient (public participation)," the Wizard explained.

Robbie hopped around the open book. "What about the private one?"

The Wizard smiled. "Private Blockchains, on the other hand, are restricted to a specific group of participants. They are controlled by an organization or consortium and offer faster and more efficient transaction processing, but with less transparency (restricted access)."

They arrived at the locked book, where a group of foxes was managing entries. "In a Private Blockchain, only authorized participants can validate transactions, making it faster and more efficient, but less open to the public (controlled validation)," the Wizard noted.

Pippa watched intently. "So, it's important to choose the right type for your needs?"

"Exactly," the Wizard replied. "Public Blockchains are ideal for situations where transparency and security are paramount, like in cryptocurrencies. Private Blockchains are better suited for organizations that need speed and efficiency while maintaining control (use cases)."

Robbie clapped his paws. "This is amazing! What else?"

The Wizard nodded. "Now, let's discuss the benefits and drawbacks of each. Public Blockchains offer high security and transparency but can be slower and resource-intensive. Private Blockchains offer speed and efficiency but require trust in the controlling entity (pros and cons)."

Barry and Robbie spent the rest of the day exploring the enchanted ledgers, amazed by their structure, operation, and impact. Even Kylie and Pippa grew more curious, asking questions and engaging with the demonstrations. By sunset, they felt enlightened and excited about the possibilities.

As they made their way back through the forest, Robbie couldn't resist mimicking the Wise Old Wizard's serious tone, causing Barry, Kylie, and Pippa to laugh.

Barry, feeling wiser and more informed, knew that with the knowledge of these technologies, they could explore and innovate in ways they had never imagined.

Explanation of Concepts

1. **Types of Blockchains**: Blockchains come in two main types—Public and Private. Public Blockchains are open to everyone, while Private Blockchains are restricted to specific participants. These types cater to different needs and use cases.
2. **Digital Ledger**: A blockchain is a digital ledger that records transactions securely and immutably. Each entry, or block, is linked to the previous one, forming a chain. This ensures that the data is accurate and tamper-proof.
3. **Decentralized Validation**: In a Public Blockchain, transactions are validated by a network of participants, ensuring no single entity controls the ledger. This decentralized approach enhances security and transparency.
4. **Transparency and Security**: Public Blockchains offer high levels of transparency and security, as anyone can participate in the validation process. However, they can be slower and require more resources to maintain.
5. **Public Participation**: Public Blockchains allow anyone to join and help maintain the ledger. This open participation makes the system highly secure but sometimes less efficient due to the need for consensus among many participants.
6. **Restricted Access**: Private Blockchains are restricted to a specific group of participants, often controlled by an organization or consortium. This restricted access allows for faster and more efficient transaction processing but with less transparency.

7. **Controlled Validation**: In a Private Blockchain, only authorized participants can validate transactions. This controlled approach offers speed and efficiency but requires trust in the entity managing the blockchain.
8. **Use Cases**: Public Blockchains are ideal for situations requiring high security and transparency, such as cryptocurrencies. Private Blockchains are suited for organizations needing fast and efficient transaction processing while maintaining control.
9. **Pros and Cons**: Public Blockchains provide security and transparency but can be slow and resource-intensive. Private Blockchains offer speed and efficiency but require trust in the controlling entity and are less open to public participation.

Questions

1. What is a blockchain?

    A. A type of enchanted book

    B. A digital ledger that records transactions in a secure and immutable way

    C. A treasure map

2. What is the key difference between Public and Private Blockchains?

    A. Public Blockchains are open to everyone, while Private Blockchains are restricted to specific participants

    B. Public Blockchains are faster than Private Blockchains

    C. Private Blockchains don't use any validation process

3. Why are Public Blockchains considered highly secure?

    A. They are controlled by a single entity

    B. They are decentralized and rely on many participants to validate transactions

    C. They don't require many resources

4. What is the main advantage of Private Blockchains over Public Blockchains?

> A. They allow for faster and more efficient transaction processing
>
> B. They are completely open to the public
>
> C. They use more resources to maintain security

5. In which scenario would a Public Blockchain be more suitable than a Private Blockchain?

> A. When an organization wants full control over the data
>
> B. When transparency and security are paramount, like in cryptocurrencies
>
> C. When transactions need to be completed as quickly as possible without concern for transparency

Answers

1. **B** - A blockchain is a digital ledger that records transactions in a secure and immutable way.
2. **A** - Public Blockchains are open to everyone, while Private Blockchains are restricted to specific participants.
3. **B** - Public Blockchains are secure because they are decentralized and rely on many participants to validate transactions.
4. **A** - Private Blockchains allow for faster and more efficient transaction processing but are restricted to authorized participants.
5. **B** - Public Blockchains are more suitable when transparency and security are essential, as in cryptocurrencies.

www.ingramcontent.com/pod-product-compliance
Lightning Source LLC
Chambersburg PA
CBHW031604210526
45464CB00004B/1429